the Bodyguard

Roy Snell

WITH LUCIAN RANDALL

ake Publishing Ltd,
2 Bramber Road,
London W14 9PB, England

www.johnblakepublishing.co.uk

First published in paperback in 2010

ISBN: 978-1-84454-838-5

British Library Cataloguing-in-Publication Data:

A catalogue record for this book is available from the British Library.

Design by www.envydesign.co.uk

Printed in Great Britain by CPI Bookmarque, Croydon, CR0 4TD

1 3 5 7 9 10 8 6 4 2

Papers used by John Blake Publishing are natural, recyclable products made from wood grown in sustainable forests. The manufacturing processes conform to the environmental regulations of the country of origin.

What makes a man a man?
Is it the house that he lives in?
Is it the car that he drives?
Is it the clothes that he wears?
Is it the amount of money he has?

It is none of these; what makes a man a man?
It is his heart!
Because even if his mind makes a decision
It is his heart that decides.

So what makes a man a man?
It is his heart.

Roy Snell
Eden Snell

CONTENTS

ACKNOWLEDGEMENTS

Thanks to:
Phil, Lee, Cliff (my brothers), Mum and my late father
and brother Steven
Sindy Bell (artist)
Lucian Randall (writer)
John Blake Publishing
Peter George Piper
Junior (the Wise Buddha)
Scott Foord (Bright Security)
Universal Music
Ann Moneypenny (my agent)

Special thanks to:
My darling wife Joanne
My darling daughters Eden and Victoria
My loving family and friends
Professor Pepper (my heart surgeon)
The unknown man who saved my life (the Guardian Angel) –
05/05/2005, Latchmere Road

A very special thank you to Pat Edmonds – if it wasn't for her, this
book would have never been published.

INTRODUCTION

Hugh Grant didn't want to take his shoes off before he was allowed to join the party but his host was Bryan Adams, a committed vegan, who won't have any leather in his home. There was only one person who could get away with breaking his strict house rule – me.

Dismayed, Hugh stood in the hallway, looking in the direction of my feet. I glared fiercely back at him. He looked in appeal towards Bryan, who shrugged and gestured back at me.

I might have been wearing a smart suit, but I'm a big bloke and I know how to intimidate, however posh the occasion. Cropped hair, sharp goatee, a voice that rattles crockery: unmistakably the gentleman in charge of the evening's security.

Bryan said, 'Are you going to tell him?'

Hugh Grant, overgrown schoolboy that he is, nodded nervously. 'Ah, yes,' he squeaked, taking his shoes off and handing them meekly to one of my boys to be stored in a rack by the door. 'I see your point.' Smart lad.

I'm a bodyguard. I've looked after the biggest stars in the world, I've taken a bullet and I've also been stabbed (twice) but I'm no hero – it's all in the line of duty. I'll lay down my life for my client. But they've got to do things my way.

I don't care who you are: Arnold Schwarzenegger, Bruce Willis, Oasis, Amy Winehouse, James Morrison or Hugh Grant, makes no difference to me, mate. Everyone gets treated the same and they respect me for it.

Over the years I've worked my way up to the top of my profession. Bryan Adams appreciated that; he knew he was totally safe. And he also knew better than to ask me to take my shoes off.

You could say attitude runs in the Snell family. All the men in my clan are big fellas, and when I first got together with my brothers to run doors in south London, we quickly earned ourselves a reputation for taking no nonsense.

But while my brothers stayed local, I became head of security for the Lyceum Theatre in the West End. It was there that I first got into personal security. I got to know all the big bands in the 1980s; I worked with the boxing fraternity. Through one of the promoters I was married to a niece of the Kray Twins for a while. Well, they said she was their niece, but they weren't properly related. Still, when Ronnie and Reggie say you're family, are you going to disagree?

It was a pretty sweet life, but then it all began to go wrong, and it was my fault. I'm not too proud to admit I started dabbling in drugs – the hard stuff, coke. I can't deny what it made me; I became everything I've always hated: a thug for hire. Cocaine brought out my darker side. I'm not saying it wasn't always in there, because it must have been part of me, but I lost control and – much more importantly – I lost all the respect I'd spent so many years building up.

I'd been a bodyguard to the stars. Now I was one of London's feared hard men: a debt-collecting lump, smashing people all over the place on the slightest pretext. Even my closest mates doubted I'd ever get back into the body-guarding world and nobody at all expected me to get right back on top again.

Me? In my worst moments I doubted it myself. It's been a long, hard journey and a lot of the time it hasn't been very pretty, but I never gave up battling.

Maybe I inherited that destructive streak from my dad – his weakness was drink, rather than drugs, but he was known for having a mean temper. And he had the build to go with it: 6'5", hands like shovels, he was 20 stone and there wasn't an inch of fat on him.

He had a battle dealing with a big, young family all on his own and then came the day when the authorities arrived to split us up. He threatened to throw the officials over the balcony of our fourth-floor flat. It was a fight they were always going to win in the end, though, and they took me and my youngest brother away and slung us in care.

I was five years old.

CHAPTER 1

BARNARDO'S BOY

My dad had been left to cope with eight children after my mum walked out on him. The oldest was Steven, then there was Phillip, Lee, Theresa, Alana, Melanie and Cliff. I was two years older than Cliff, having been born on 4 November 1961.

I'd been a sickly baby, lots of breathing disorders and glandular fever kept me in hospital for 18 months, but then life was all pretty happy – at least for those first few years. Then my mum, Rose Evans, left.

The authorities decided that my dad, Jim Snell, couldn't look after eight children alone and the younger four were to be taken into care. Just like that.

Dad's brother Ron knew there would be trouble when they came. He'd seen Dad's short fuse at first hand. It got him slung out of the police force, which you might say had been the family firm. My grandfather, James Snell, was 32 years a copper in the City of London. His wife, Elizabeth, had been an inspector before leaving to become secretary to none other than Prime Minister Harold Macmillan. Uncle Ron served in the Royal Marines before he too became a copper. He was transferred into the Special

Branch and featured in a *Panorama* programme when he was involved in capturing a high-profile paedophile.

Dad, born James Snell in 1938, had been in the RAF for some time and it was while training as a sparkie (an electrician) that he approached Ron about getting into the police. We never really got the full story of what went wrong; Dad never talked about it while he was alive.

The family story goes that Dad was a PC when he and Ron, by then a plain clothes detective sergeant, were called to a block of flats where a guy had murdered his baby by smashing it against the wall head-first.

'It wouldn't stop crying,' shouted the suspect. 'So I had to shut it up, the fucking thing drove me mad!'

And Dad, thinking of all the kids he was looking after on his own, chinned the geezer, knocking him spark out. That was the end of his career in the old bill, and it was only a few weeks later that the letter came to say that he wasn't able to cope with bringing up eight kids on his own. The two youngest girls, and me and my brother Cliff, were going to have to go into Barnardo's.

Ron offered to help the authorities make it go a little easier. He saw to it that old bill lined the corridors and stairs in the flats. Ron himself knocked on the door and tried to calm things down, but Dad was effing and blinding, and trying to take a swing at the coppers. Cliffy and me were dragged away to a Barnardo's home. For the next five years we spent our time with a series of foster parents, sometimes for periods of under two weeks.

We were uncontrollable: we couldn't understand why we weren't with Dad; we knew that us kids were his whole world and we were angry all the time. And sometimes it was like the authorities deliberately tried to make things harder for us by giving us families who were guaranteed to wind us up.

Like the Sandersons. Middle-aged, with a girl three years older than me and a boy a year older than Cliffy, they had a beautiful house, loads of money and their own kids were well turned out. They put up with our constant shoplifting, ducking off school and getting into scraps.

But they were so religious!

I'd never been in a church in my life and that wasn't about to change when I saw what they'd got for me and my brother to wear for our first visit: knee-length, grey shorts. White shirts with a pattern down the front and short sleeves. Long white socks! And sandals! All of them wore the same thing – they looked like the von Trapp family.

'Bollocks to that!' I said to Cliff.

We changed into jeans and T-shirts – Cliff had his Arsenal strip on – and went downstairs to see what they were going to do about it. Mr Sanderson tried to reason with us, but we weren't having any of it. So he told us that if we didn't look the part, we'd have to stay in the house. Suited us. So we spent the next eight months of Sundays locked in our room. Maybe they hoped that we would find Jesus in there.

All I did was find a way out: a drainpipe running by the window, which overlooked the back garden. Sturdy-looking, cast iron drainpipe... Perfect.

'C'mon, bruv,' I said. 'We're going.' I climbed out the window first and shinned down to the bottom.

'It's a bit fuckin' high, innit, Roy?' Cliff called down after me. He was only six, but he was quite right. I hadn't even thought about it when I swung out, but when I came to look up, I realised I must have come down about four storeys. So I tried to reassure Cliffy.

'Just look at the wall,' I shouted. 'Don't look down, you'll be all right, mate.' Good as gold, he did as I said. Halfway down, I saw the whole pipe start to sway. Cliff felt it and froze.

'Did the drainpipe move?' came this nervous little voice.

'No, no – of course not! Just keep going.'

He was still 25 foot up in the air when, screeching in protest, the pipe started to pull away from the wall. A length of guttering came with it and the whole lot hung in the air as if uncertain which way to fall. I didn't want to be under it when it finally made up its mind and took off as soon as it tumbled towards me.

Cliff took a desperate leap for safety. Fortunately for him, he had a nice, soft landing – me! I staggered to my feet, wheezing, but unharmed. Which was more than you could say for the garden.

Mr Sanderson was proud of the results of his green-fingered efforts, but that was before the outside had been redecorated with fragments of pipe, gutter and tile. Crunched-up brick doesn't do much for your flowers and several gnomes were no more. One of the fences was completely wiped out. Time to do a runner.

We made a break for the greenhouse that stood by a garden wall. It was intact and Cliff gave me a leg-up; I knelt on the edge to pull him up. Near the top he slipped from my grasp and I fell backwards through the glass, landing on my back, covered in shards and cut to ribbons. I tried to stand up, but I'd slashed my foot badly. Claret everywhere.

The Sandersons rushed me to hospital and soon I was bandaged up, but their Christian forgiveness had been comprehensively exhausted.

They were going to send us back to Barnardo's.

Fuck that! In the confusion back at the partially-wrecked house, we gathered up our possessions in a carrier bag and escaped – this time by the front door. Free!

We were young and we were on our own, but we were sure it had to be better than what we'd left behind.

But I hadn't realised quite how late it was.

It was getting dark and I was starting to panic when at last we came to some allotments by a railway line. We broke into a shed. Inside, we found a light, blankets and a big barrel of fresh water so we settled down for our first night on the run.

The next morning we were absolutely starving. We had no money and we hadn't thought to take any provisions. We walked out to the main road and found a petrol station run by an old geezer who would shuffle out to fill up the tanks, wipe car windows and chat to the customers. In the process, he'd leave his shop unattended for minutes at a time.

Long enough for us to nip in and nick a kids' banquet – milk, biscuits, bags of crisps, pork pies, fags and some matches, enough to keep our adventure going.

Day three and the novelty of being outlaws had worn off. We'd eaten all the food by the evening and we hated the prospect of having to wake up on the floor, cold and stiff. And we had to wait another night until the garage was open.

While the old fella was preoccupied with a tanker on the forecourt making a delivery of petrol, I told Cliff to be lookout and ran in to rummage round the back. There, I found loads of boxes of sweets stacked up. Bingo! But we could only manage to drag one each all the way back to the shed.

Stomachs rumbling so loud you could hear them

halfway down the railway line, we ripped open the boxes.

Wine gums. That's all that was in those boxes. *Wine gums*.

Oh, well. We were hungry enough. We must have scoffed so many family-sized packets of wine gums, I'm surprised we weren't pissed, but we couldn't risk going back to the petrol station a second time that day.

We made two important discoveries during our research into the effects of a wine gum-based diet. One: they don't stop you feeling hungry, even if you eat them for four days straight. Two: they really stop up your arse.

By the end of the week, Cliff was curled up on the floor, convinced he was about to die. He howled helplessly and I made up my mind that we would have to give ourselves up and get him to a hospital. You should have seen the look on his face. The physical pain was nothing compared to the terror of going back to the God-fearing Sandersons. He looked like he was about to shit himself – which, under the circumstances, was not such a bad reaction.

'No, no, no! They'll send us back,' he wailed. 'We can't!' And then his eyes widened with something more than terror. It looked like the fear had solved his medical dilemma.

He leapt to his feet and dashed out of the shed. I couldn't begin to describe the noises that drifted back into our little bolthole but when he came back, he was a changed boy. His colour returned, he was breathing normally. And he was fucking hungry again! We both were, so we decided to take our chances and move on the next day.

Cliffy slept like a baby that night, but then I suppose the poor little kid was little more than that in truth. I fretted about what we were going to do next. Whatever that involved, it wouldn't be the remains of the wine gums.

All we packed the next morning was Cliff's football and

our carrier bag of possessions. We set off over the railway track and headed across the field on the far side. I was still limping, the stitches from my cuts well overdue for an inspection. The bandages were filthy.

We got halfway across the field and could see a stream in front of us – but I could hear something too, a thundering sound. I glanced over my shoulder. Charging towards us, nostrils flared, legs pounding, was a bull about the size of a double-decker bus! I grabbed Cliff around his waist, kicked his precious ball over the stream and pulled him along with me towards the safety of a cattle grid just beyond the bridge.

Cliff heard the hooves, looked around and froze in sheer terror – causing me, holding onto him, to lose my footing and tumble into the stream. I clambered onto the far bank. But Cliff had no chance: he was about to find himself on the end of a sharp pair of horns. And still he stood, transfixed.

'*Cliffy!*'

It broke the spell. He looked over at me, started to move, fell over and ended up under the bridge.

The bull realised it was heading straight for the water. He tried to put the anchors on, but it was too late. With clouds of dust billowing up around him, he slammed into the side of the bridge and skidded over the bank. Ever seen a bull do a cartwheel? It's an awe-inspiring sight. It landed on its back in the water. The banks of the stream were too narrow for the bull to turn and right itself, so it lay there, screaming and churning up the sides with its horns.

Cliffy, waist-high in mud, was inches away from the beast's rolling eyes and steam-train snorts. It gave us a look that seemed to say: 'Some day I'll get you for this!'

I pulled Cliff out of the stream and we started running.

We could still hear furious bull noises, even as we neared the hedgerow on the other end of the field. Convinced it would free itself and try to make good on its threat, we dived through the hedge and rolled onto the pavement on the other side, right in front of a local copper. Our disappearance had sparked a full-scale search and life on the run ended in an exhausted heap by the side of the road.

We were marched back to Barnardo's, who were beginning to despair that they would ever be able to do anything with us. For a while they tried various sorts of punishments, separations and forfeits, and sent us to a parade of caseworkers, child psychologists and social workers. In the end, what did it for us was the simplest solution of all: we were sent to someone who was quite nice.

Irene had been a widow for two years. She was in her early 50s, had never been able to have children of her own and accepted us, despite our bad press. We couldn't believe she was for real. Sweet-natured, she did everything she could to be a proper mum.

She loved cooking and we'd wake up in the morning to the smell of freshly-baked bread waiting for us on the breakfast table. Lovely. The first time we stared at it, like it was a priceless family heirloom.

'Well, take a slice,' said Irene. Cliff looked at her suspiciously, expecting a clump.

'What? How do you mean?'

'Go on! I made it for you.' It was real butter. Best thing ever.

Irene would take us for days out and give us treats for no particular reason. She wasn't even wealthy, but she just wanted to do her best. She even hired a colour telly so that we could watch footy and *Doctor Who*. And in return we didn't mind having to take our shoes off and wash our hands and faces as soon as we got in. That would have amazed some of the other people we stayed with – but then some of them would have been surprised to see us come back at all.

We were put into a specialist school which looked after kids with behavioural problems and it was the first time I ever got anywhere with education. I found out that I was good at maths and I liked reading and history as well. The school was encouraging and made me want to go in every day; I even had extra lessons on a Saturday. Within six months, I became a completely different boy.

And then came the letter from the social services. My three older brothers had left home and Dad could have us four younger kids back.

Much as we liked Irene, we wanted to be with the rest of our family and when Dad turned up, all three of us burst into tears. We hadn't seen each for years. We hugged and Irene discreetly disappeared off to the kitchen to get us a cake for the journey. Already, we'd almost forgotten her.

Dad had a Zephyr 6 and I bounced up and down on the back seat in excitement at the thought of going home at last. We drove off without saying much of a goodbye to Irene, to be honest. I have often wondered what happened to her; she was so good to us, but we never contacted her again. I think we were afraid of showing our emotions, but it was sad that we cut her out of our lives.

Our real family still lived in south London, in a massive house in Sudbourne Road off Brixton Hill. By the time I saw it, I was eleven years old and my brother was nine; we couldn't even remember what the rest of the kids looked like.

We were told that the older boys had gone off the rails. Steve was a rogue and was often in fights. So was Lee. He was a fraudster – he used to fake Post Office book stamps, got into heroin and almost died. He was staying away from Dad because he knew he didn't approve of his lifestyle.

Phil was settled down with a partner, Lynnie, and had two kids, Tracy and Kelly. He worked in the scrap-yard just around the corner and we would soon get to see more of him and the yard than we did of school – and that would cause me a lot of trouble in the years to come.

Theresa was still living at home and we saw Melanie and Alana for the first time. We were all in tears. The two youngest girls had done all right in care: they had ended up in a beautiful home with a proper family, down by the coast in Havent, and they seemed to have had a much better time of it than us.

By then Dad was with his new wife, Judy – and now we were once more a family.

CHAPTER 2

ON THE RUN

I was thirteen and I had no intention of going to school. I'd been looking after me and Cliff for so long – I just wanted to earn money. We enrolled in a local school, but most of the time we were grafting.

Phil knew I'd never be forced into education at school. He taught me how to drive and I had a Ford Popular when most kids were playing in the park.

I even told Dad I wanted to live in my own place – but he wouldn't have any of it.

With a nod from his boss, I drove a lorry from Phil's scrap-yard to the main dump in Wandsworth. I enjoyed it; I was fourteen at the time.

Things at home didn't stay quite so good. Dad lost the place in Sudbourne Road and we had to move from Brixton to Lavender Hill, ending up in a smaller place above a launderette. I got a job in the chip shop, but Dad was getting letters galore from the school authorities.

'You have to go,' he told me.

So I enrolled in Kingsdale, 5 miles back south towards Crystal Palace. Once again, the chances of making it into school on a daily basis were slim. We had to get two buses, one of which went past the scrap-yard – and that was it for me.

I left the house in my school uniform and changed into my work jumper at the bus stop. Phil would try to get us to go on to school but I just said, 'Nah, can't be arsed.'

The boss would pull into the playground in our HGV class 3 and I'd stroll into the classroom and say to Mr Davis the teacher, 'I'm here.'

I assumed the truancy officials would never find out if I signed the register.

Mr Davis would take one look at the state of me in my grubby work clothes and comment, 'I take it you're not staying?' But he didn't try to stop me as I made my mark, walked out of school and jumped back into the lorry. Then it was back to work for me.

We drove zinc and copper to a big dump at Wandsworth. You weighed the lorry on the industrial scales, dropped off the load, re-weighed the empty vehicle and were paid for the difference.

Our crafty boss would have got us to fill lead pipes with water and then bash the ends down so it was heavier – which meant more money. If Cliffy, a small lad, was with us, he'd be asked to hide in the cab while they did the first weigh and then jump out the second time. Every little helped.

I used to get paid £10.50 a week, a lot of money in those days. Out of it, I would give my dad a fiver each week and he went across to the pub and drank the lot. He was becoming an alcoholic and would try to get us into whiskey too, staggering home after closing and telling us, 'Yeah, have some of that. It'll put hairs on your chest.'

It was disgusting! We all really hated it when he did that.

And he was getting nastier in other ways – he would use the buckle end of his belt for even the tiniest misdemeanour.

But he couldn't make me go to school, no matter how many letters he received from the authorities. And still they kept on writing.

It couldn't go on forever; even I should have guessed that. And yet I never dreamed of how hard they were going to crack down when they eventually came for us.

Old bill turned up at the scrap-yard.

Phil was on his way out and I could have made things a whole lot worse as I was just climbing into the driver's seat of the lorry. But the police didn't even look at me. They looked straight at my youngest brother and asked, 'Are you Clifford?'

Cliffy went, 'Yeah?'

'Why aren't you at school?' asked one of the officers.

''Cos I'm working!'

Phil piped up, 'He's not feeling well.' Not the most plausible excuse ever.

'What do you mean, "He's not feeling well?"' said the police officer. 'If he's not feeling well, what's he doing here? He's gotta come with us.'

And they took Cliffy away.

Didn't even *look* at me! Didn't give me a second look. I was barely fifteen, but I could pass for years older after all the physical graft I'd been doing. My escape made me think they were never going to get me. Wrong.

Cliff was given a date for his court appearance and I just kept on for the rest of the week as normal. Didn't change a thing.

It got to the Friday, what we called the 'clear day', when all the scrap metal was separated into piles in preparation for taking the big load to the dump, which we did every

Saturday. Two more old bill pitched up while I was in the middle of my duties: one had stripes, the other looked aggressive. *Good cop, bad cop*. Didn't scare me!

'I ain't going nowhere,' I said flatly.

'You do as you're told,' said the nasty-looking one.

I was still holding a piece of piping I'd been about to add to the pile of lead before I'd been so rudely interrupted. Back then, I was foolish and hot-headed, and I meant it when I said, 'You come near me and I'll stick this across your nut.'

That was it. Bad cop started towards me, but suddenly I felt myself being grabbed by Phil from behind. He knew damn well I had every intention of smashing the copper over the head with it.

Pinning my arms to my side, he said, 'Listen, listen, you don't do that! Calm yourself down.'

'They ain't taking me nowhere,' I told him angrily.

I was fuming. Phil even offered to follow them down to the nick in his car, but they weren't having any of it. While he still held me, they pounced, put the handcuffs on me and took me down to Brixton nick. I was stuck there until late at night – but when I did finally get out, I had no idea how short-lived my freedom was to be.

The following Monday I had to appear in court. I was still not much over fourteen and, although it was true that I hadn't exactly been what you might call a regular at school, I was honestly expecting a bit of a slap across the wrists, at least a second chance, so I was stunned when the judge told me what they were going to do with me.

I was going to go to Borstal for two years.

Jesus Christ, I thought. *That was a bit of a liberty!*

I then I remembered I'd forgotten to pick up my wages on the Friday. That was what made me most angry!

So I was sent to Stamford House in Shepherd's Bush, but I wasn't going to stay there. They had no chance.

Like a regular school, Stamford was subdivided into four smaller units, or houses: Peckham, O'Hare, Hastings and Churchill, each with their own colour. I was assigned to Peckham, which meant I had to wear a blue jumper with a black stripe.

Peckham was reserved for boys who could have a row and the staff were picked because they could also handle themselves. Our teacher looked like he might have been a double for a mountain: he was huge, with hands like shovels. And everything else was in proportion – his arms were massive, even his head was enormous. His name was Ron Ellis. He let it be known that if you wanted to have a row, you would have a row with Ron, a proper one.

He'd put the gloves on and growl, 'C'mon, then. Let's have you.' But I didn't plan to be around long enough to try out.

Four days in, I was being marched across the yard and I noticed the gates didn't have barbed wire across the top. That was all I needed. I sprinted, *bang!* Straight over the gate, before they even knew what was happening, I was gone.

I didn't have a pot to piss in and I was on my toes.

So I decided to go to my brother Phil's in Christchurch Road, off Brixton Hill in Streatham. Hardly the best place to go if the entire borstal service was out looking for me, but I didn't think about that. I pretended to have lost my bus money when the conductor came up. I kept getting thrown off buses; it took me hours to get to Phil's and it wasn't even such a long way across London. And I hardly had a chance to raise my hand to knock on the door before old bill grabbed me from behind. They'd been waiting for me.

Straight back to Stamford House, slung in the punishment cell: you didn't get anything in there. No blankets, no mattress, no pillow. Just a wooden bench and 24 hours to make you think about what you'd done.

The next day, I was taken back to Peckham House with two prison officers flanking me, just in case I decided to make a dash for it again. Another group of inmates marched the other way – and to my surprise, there was my brother Cliff with them. It turned out he had been sentenced to two years as well.

''Ello, bruv,' he called out as they strode past.

''Ello, son,' I replied.

He was in being held in Churchill, but I wasn't having us separated and so I went and had a word with Ron Ellis. You had to ask permission for absolutely everything in that place and after I'd asked for permission to speak, I told him I wanted Cliffy to be in the same unit. He said he'd see what he could do. Some of the screws could be really nasty and I had no idea if Ron was one who would honour his promise, but the very next day, my brother arrived at Peckham. Ron called me over.

'Snell, here, front forward. I've just done you the biggest favour. Now you owe me. Don't forget it.'

'No, Mr Ellis.'

'Jolly good.' And that was it. And I thought, *well, he's not a bad fella.* He did do what he said he would do and in return I had to stay out of trouble, which I managed to do for a whole two days. Then someone nicked my fags.

Everyone was allowed to smoke, even us under-sixteens. Each inmate had their own tobacco tin with their name on it and in the evening – 'Permission to smoke, sir?' – a screw would chuck us over the material. I kept half a bag of baccy in my room so I could have a crafty fag outside whenever I wanted. It was hidden in a bag, which was nicked out of my cell.

Fuming, I had half a mind I knew who'd done it too. He was a big lump, east European or Russian, something like that, called Rudzinski. We called him Russ because we could pronounce it.

A bully, Russ was the petty type who would go around taking the cues off people when they wanted to play snooker. I found him, but soon forgot all about the stolen cigarettes. He had my brother Cliffy pinned up by his head against the wall in the games room.

I went for him.

There were a couple of screws in the room but I didn't care who was watching by that point. I picked up one of the cues and whacked it so hard over Russ's nut that the cue snapped. He went down like a sack of shit just as the screws got to us.

I put my hands up to show that I was going to come quietly, but one of them just punched me straight in the face.

I wasn't going to have that!

I absolutely battered him. He was a fully-grown adult, but I was pretty fit. I smashed him all over the gaff. But the other screw wasn't a rucker: give him his due he calmed me down. Big Ron Ellis soon arrived on the scene.

There was me, stood in the middle of the games room, still fuming, and I was flanked by bodies – Russ spark out one side, the screw on the other.

For a moment, Ron surveyed the carnage.

'Do I have to carry you, or are you going to walk?' he asked.

I looked him in the eye as I began to think things through. 'Every man has got to know his limits,' I told him straight, 'and you've just walked in.'

Ron wasn't a man known for his sense of humour: I don't think he'd even been known to crack a smile, but he burst out laughing.

'Come on, son,' he said, not unkindly. 'You know what you've got to do.'

We started walking towards the punishment cell. He asked what had happened in the games room and I told him how I'd been provoked. It was an uneasy moment. I'd just beaten up one of his screws and I was sure big Ron was going to beat the shit out of me when nobody else was watching.

'Hmm...' was all he said. 'I probably would have done the same, son,' and with that he shut the punishment cell door behind me. Then I knew that guy was all right; he wasn't a bully. I learned respect from Ron.

After two days, I was let out of the cell and arrested for causing actual and grievous bodily harm. GBH was for Russ and ABH for the screw. The trial was held inside Stamford House and my two-year sentence was extended by 18 months. *Looking at quite a bit of bird here,* I thought. *I'm not staying here for all that time.* So I started working out how I could get on my toes.

I looked for other weak points in the security. It wasn't long before I'd come up with quite a plan – it was quite sophisticated for a kid my age. Behind our living quarters was wire-mesh fencing and beyond that, a block of flats. I guessed I could get through the fence with bolt cutters.

I'd need to climb through a window at the back of the communal area. A guy in the workshop got me a piece of metal, with which I bent back the bar on the window. It used to stick anyway, so nobody ever tried to open it and it went unnoticed that the bar was out of shape.

I told my brother I was off. 'Listen, mate,' I warned him. 'I've gotta go, I *have* to go. I don't care.' He knew me well enough to understand.

The shifts changed over in the evening, giving me a half-hour to get out. Soon I was squeezing myself through the window, which I then shut carefully and quietly behind me. I ran to the fence and started to cut through the mesh; I wasn't seen and it wasn't long before I was able to push open a section. Then I was away – and this time I had even thought to bring some money with me as well.

I had learned enough to realise that the police would be at my family's home again so I ended up sleeping rough on Clapham Common, not far from my brother's in south London. It wasn't easy out there; I really came to understand what it felt like to be homeless. You've just got the clothes on your back and not only are you exposed to the elements, but I've got to say, you get some right fucking freaks coming out of a night-time! But I just told myself that it was better than being in prison for the next three-and-a-half years.

Towards Clapham South tube there was a bit of woodland next to a pond, where geezers go night fishing. I saw a fire: Heat! *A kettle.*

So I wandered over, pretending that I was also fishing and that my tent and rod had been nicked. Straightaway, I got a cup of tea from the owner of the kettle and he even offered me a sandwich. I didn't want to take his food, but he insisted. Blinding! I was starving.

But it was a freezing cold winter. I had to keep walking around to stay warm and after a while, found an alleyway that was out of the wind. Peering over one of the walls, I could see someone's washing on the line. *A coat*! I jumped over, nicked it and escaped back to the common.

It was when I tried on my new possession that I realised I'd only gone and stolen some bird's coat! The sleeves came up to my elbows, but you know what? I couldn't have cared less. It was my blanket – but even with it on, I could still feel the bitter temperature. I dug myself into the wooded area of the common's south side as best I could, burying myself under leaves to insulate me from the worst of the night.

Early on the fifth morning of my life on the run, I left my woodland bedroom just as a police car was cruising by. I must have looked a complete sight. It pulled up and I gave them a moody name and address, which of course they checked over the radio.

'Look, we're going to ask you again,' they said, 'and if you don't tell us, we're going to take you in, simple as that.'

I knew I was stuffed, so I gave them my real name.

'You know you're wanted,' they said.

'Yeah, yeah, yeah,' I sighed. I knew what was coming and I was half-relieved.

'You going to give us any aggro?'

'Not at all.' To be honest, I was so cold, I was so tired and I was so hungry, I just thought, *you know what? I give up*. I was ready to go back and face the punishment.

Stamford House wasn't going to take me back for a third time. Now I was off to Latchmere House, further out south.

A proper Young Prison (YP), as secure as an adult open prison. Another six months added to my sentence. There was only one thing to do – escape again.

So I became a trustee – meaning I got to wear a yellow band and have a job in the steam room, doing all the sheets and blankets. We filled massive bags with laundry, which would be taken out by a van. You can guess where this is going.

I smuggled myself into one of the loads of washing, covered in bags. That was the easy bit. But I knew that I still had to deal with the guy who unloaded the van. I'd had some help inside the laundry room, but the van driver knew nothing of his stowaway. He opened the doors and I braced myself to be uncovered.

'Come and see the Consul, mate,' said a voice. *Someone was talking to the driver!* 'I've had it all sprayed now.' They walked off to admire the newcomer's Ford, leaving the van doors open. Well, why wouldn't they?

So I pushed the bags off, struggled out of the laundry bag, dropped out the back of the van and walked away. I nicked a motor to get back to south London.

For the next three weeks it was the same as before: sleeping rough and going into shops to nick food. Fucking hungry, all the time. I couldn't think of anything else.

So I didn't even see the panda car filling up at the petrol station forecourt: I was too busy running away with the sandwiches I'd just grabbed from the fridge by the cash desk. I almost fell over the copper. He only needed to open his arms to catch me.

'Oh... I was *so* hungry,' I said by way of explanation.

'Never mind bloody hungry, you thieving little shit!' he said, not knowing that I really hadn't eaten properly for weeks. He took the sandwiches for evidence and by the time we got to the station, they'd found out my full story.

'God almighty!' said the copper. 'Wouldn't you be better off staying where you bloody were?' As he was talking, he was bagging up the food and said to the desk sergeant, 'Exhibit one: prawn sandwich.'

'*Prawn?*' I yelled. *I don't fucking eat prawns.* The other one was even worse – crab with some kind of dressing. *I hate crab even more.* Even the coppers started laughing.

I was now a high-risk prisoner: I had a temper, a record of assaults and I'd escaped from two establishments – and all in the space of a year. This time they sent me to Ashford Young Prison, with uniformed screws and proper cells. It backed onto the adult prison in a deliberate attempt to make you realise where you would end up if you kept on the way you were going. Both sides of the nick were run by the same staff and had the same guv'nor.

Just the other side of the bars, you could see the adult lags, among them a Charlie Smith, who had committed murder with an axe. When he was later released, he would go on to do another two from the same family and ended up in Broadmoor. The geezer was properly ill.

As I was coming out of my cell, I heard him shout, 'Oi! Think you're hard, do ya? I can't wait to meet you this side! We'll see how tough you really are then.' The screws deliberately organised these encounters to try and warn us off carrying on the same way and ending up in the adult part of the prison.

I still had three years to go on my sentence. This time, I decided, I would just get on with it and do it, but as soon as I was seventeen, the Guv'nor asked to see me.

'You're going to be released next Thursday,' he announced. For a moment, I thought I was going to be transferred somewhere else; I couldn't believe it. It turned out that the law had just been changed so that you could get out after serving a third of your sentence. 'I do not wish to see you back here again...' he continued, with the usual speech.

I left with £5.70 that I'd saved while working in the prison, and they gave me £4 and a packed lunch. It was a lovely summer's day in 1977 and I felt fantastic.

Back in Brixton, I went into a baker's to get something

to eat, just as a police car pulled up, and I froze, I just froze. Habit, I guess.

I just went, 'Yeah, it's me. I'm here.' The copper looked at me.

'What do you mean by that?' Then I realised they really weren't after me.

'I've just been released, I promise you; I haven't escaped. I really have been released.'

Now I was babbling.

But that didn't have the effect of reassuring the copper. They were just answering a call round the corner, but once I blurted all that out they had to check up on who I was. Of course, they couldn't help but remind me my sentence was still open and that I had to stay out of trouble.

I became determined to make something out of my life.

With nowhere else to go, I had to start back at Dad's. Cliffy, then fourteen, served out his sentence quietly and was back at school where he was doing well. Judy said Dad was at the pub every night: he was a full-blown alcoholic.

It was her that I felt most sorry for. I'd always thought of Judy as my mum after I came back from Barnardo's because my real mother had done so little for us.

I knew the other members of my family were still seeing our real mother, but for a long time I just refused. It was only after a lot of convincing that I relented – and it was very tense when we did get together for the first time. I didn't recognise her at first. She had very dark hair and looked Italian. I didn't realise that her full name was Roselle Alicia Evans. She'd taken her second name and shortened it, introducing herself as Alex.

'Sorry,' I muttered, 'I was looking for Rose Evans.'

'That's me, you silly sod,' she said. 'You must be my Royston.' That was the first time I knew my own full name was Royston.

'Christ,' I said. 'That must mean you must be my biological mother?'

'Well, yes, if you have to put it in that formal way,' she said. 'I see your father's poisoned you.'

'He's not done anything. I've only just come out of prison.'

'Why? What stupid things have you been doing? I never would have brought you up that way.'

'Well, you didn't bring me up at all,' I said flatly. 'So, why are you talking about it?'

Then I got to hear her side of why she left Dad. At first I wasn't sure that I could believe anything she said after so long, but when she told me that he'd been drinking even back then, I suddenly started paying very close attention.

As far as I knew, he'd only recently become a serious boozer and I hadn't mentioned that to her. My mind raced. Maybe the boozing had only just come to the surface? Could it be true?

I didn't know if she was telling the truth, but I wanted to hear more.

'I was cooking while you were in the garden with your brother and your sisters,' she said. 'He came in drunk, and he decided he didn't like what was on the stove and he picked up a pan of potatoes in boiling water and lobbed it at me.'

Out of sheer fright, she told me, she picked up a carving knife and said she'd stab him if he came near her. Dad grabbed the iron and moved towards her. She stuck him with the knife. He chucked the iron, she ducked and the iron crashed straight through the window into the garden, where we were playing.

The moment she said that, something triggered deep within me. I thought to myself, *I remember that crash*. She looked surprised when I told her. I was only four when it happened. And yet... my vague memory supported her version of events. If it was true, it meant that she hadn't left in the way we'd been told. Everything was different. I found it hard to process.

I still felt very loyal to Jude – Dad's second wife. For a long time I stayed with them, but in the end I decided to give Mum a go. Dad agreed that I should make up my own mind and alternated between her and him.

But then he blew it.

He'd come back late one night pissed as a fucking fart and in one of his foul tempers. When Judy brought his dinner in, he went, 'What the fucking hell is that shit?' He knocked it straight out of her hands and it went all over the floor. *It was just like the story my real mother had told me.*

I was furious. 'What the fuck is your problem? Look at the state of you, what's the matter with you?'

'Who the fuck...' he started.

'Shut up!' I told him. 'You're not going to bully me anymore. I'm not going to take your shit, Dad. You've got to get your act together.'

He gave a drunken laugh and slurred, 'Go and live with your fucking slag of a mother...'

'The trouble with you,' I said, 'is you don't know when to quit. Uncle Ron would be disgusted with you.' I told Cliffy he could come with me, if he wanted. *Cliff didn't need to stay with that fucking muppet!*

Dad stood in the doorway as I made to leave.

'I ain't going to be spoken to like that by you, you little runt,' he said.

And he went for me, but he was too slow and too pissed. Two quick punches and he hit the floor. Out cold, sparko.

Judy was crying.

I told her, 'When he wakes up, tell him from me that I

don't want to see him.' I walked out of the house and I didn't speak to Dad for the next four years. But maybe I did some good: I kept in touch with Jude and she said that he never laid a hand on her again.

It seemed like a good moment to make a completely fresh start. As it happened, Rose had moved out of London to Northamptonshire and the idea of getting out of the London scene entirely appealed to me and to Cliffy, so we decided to join her.

CHAPTER 3

MILITARY MAN

The sergeant glanced down at me in the mud, blood streaming down my face and grinned sadistically.

'Having a little lie-down, are we?'

He knew he'd made a mistake as soon as I stood up. I lost it and before he could back off, I'd already smashed him in the face. He was straight down – broken jaw, broken cheekbone. I was ready to finish him off, but four of my mates grabbed me. It was too late.

I'd hardly started training with the 7th Royal Anglian when I got into trouble. The sergeant was a bully called Socket and he never liked me. He'd been selected to join the SAS Reserves and he thought he had something to prove; he was always on my case.

We had to carry kit over a river and he made sure he gave me the massive machine gun, which weighed a fucking ton. I had to keep it dry while pulling myself across the river by a rope secured on the other side. Already I'd lugged the gun for miles across muddy terrain, over barbed wire and up and down endless hills. I was knackered.

Young and full of piss and vinegar, I just thought, *Roy,*

you've come this far. It's only a fucking river! I wasn't going to let it beat me, so I inched across on my back with the full weight of the weapon on my chest and I'd almost got to the other side when I caught a glimpse of Socket deliberately letting the rope go slack. Headfirst I went, into the muddy bank, smashing my head against the weapon, and then I sent him off to military hospital.

But provocation is no excuse in the forces, and I knew it: you just don't do that to your superiors.

The Military Police held me overnight in the cells. The next morning I was brought before the Commanding Officer and told that I was out of the Marines. It had been my dream to serve with them, but now I didn't care. *Fuck 'em*, I thought. I felt the anger still coursing through my body, the adrenaline... but it didn't last.

Back in Brixton, at my brother's place, the full implications of what I'd done began to sink in. All that hard work, passion and dedication had gone with my temper. I realised that I'd thrown away a once-in-a-lifetime opportunity; my uncle Ron had encouraged me all the way and he would be furious when he found out how badly I'd let myself down. I'd made a massive mistake.

When I lived with my real mum in Northamptonshire, I'd started training as a fighter. I'd heard there was a boxing gym in her town, nothing special, but I thought I'd take a look. The trainer was a Jamaican bloke called Akai, who gave me some gloves and invited me to have a go with one of his fighters.

I could handle myself in a street fight, but I'd never had any formal training. My dad had a reputation for being a bit of brawler, to the point where he'd get money for taking people on in pubs. If someone fancied their chances, the two of them would go out the back of the pub and have a bare-knuckle punch-up for a fiver, but that was about as professional as it got. This was new territory for me.

'Get in there, move around,' Akai said, before turning to my opponent. 'Take it easy, just do ducking and weaving.' He obviously didn't expect much from me as he rang the bell and his geezer came out, dancing and showing off, leaving himself totally exposed.

What's the matter with him? Eventually, the fella got round to coming close enough to do something useful, but before he could do so, I just hit him with one punch and down he went. *Oops, sorry!*

'What's all that dancing-about stuff with him?' I asked Akai. 'If you're gonna fight, fight! Don't just prance about.' Akai looked devastated. I'd just knocked out his heavyweight, the best fighter in his gym, and he couldn't believe I'd had no formal training. He told me I was a natural and suggested I take it up properly.

I was amazed – I'd never given what I did any thought at all, but the very next day he started to teach me. His own son, Suki, was my first sparring partner, a light heavyweight. He was big and a serious bloke – he looked like a heavyweight and his dad reckoned he could go all the way.

One thing was for sure – Suki was nothing like the bloke I'd fought the day before. He hardly moved his arms; he just looked at me, trying to psych me out. He kept coming up to me, feinting and making me flinch back. In the end I just thought that one of us had to make a move, so I landed a punch on his head and he started to come back at me. Feet against the ropes, he bombarded me with punches that found my ribs, again and again.

Akai was enjoying it. He called out, 'Are you going to hit him back, or are you just planning to stand there all day?' I managed to land a punch with my left and as Suki came back at me, he dropped his own left hand. That was all I needed. I went through the undefended middle with one devastating punch. He went down on his arse.

'*Jesus!*' said his dad, astonished for the second time in as many days. 'I've seen people fight hard before, but you hit like a freight train. I want you to train with me properly.'

There was a lot for me to learn.

I had no style, I was just a slugger, but within six weeks Akai got me to the point where I could fight on an amateur bill. My first opponent was Tony Blacksock from Daventry, in Northampton. It was a proper fight – we had blue shirts and had to wear headguards and mouthpieces. Suki went first and he won. Dave Cook was another of Akai's fighters and he also won. Then I was up. Ringside was Terry Downes, former Middleweight Champion of the World, and the judge was John Conti. My first fight was about to begin, but I didn't get much of a chance to be excited about it. From bell to 10-second count via Blacksock hitting the floor was a grand total of 13 seconds. It had taken me just two punches.

'He was fucking good, weren't he?' I heard Terry Downes say.

And that winning streak just continued – 14 fights straight, each one a knockout. Never got cut, never got put down; the only damage was having a few teeth knocked out.

But it wasn't enough. Being a boxer wasn't enough to fulfil me.

So what was I going to do? I'd never got anything out of school – I'd hardly even been there long enough, even if they'd wanted to take the time to teach me something useful. I had no idea what I was going to do. Uncle Ron took charge.

Ron had worked his way up to being a police inspector.

He'd watched with concern as I seemed to be drifting the same way as my dad. The two brothers didn't really get on then, though towards the end of their lives they would become inseparable. Over a coffee in London, Ron and I ended up meeting about my future.

It wasn't hard to get back down to the capital. I had a Zephyr 6 by then, like Dad's old car. And – though it might come as a surprise, given my early years at the scrap-yard – it was taxed, insured and it had an MOT. Although, if I'm completely honest, I hadn't quite got a licence yet, so all the paperwork was in my brother's name. That made it completely worthless, of course, but somehow I felt a bit better doing it that way.

Ron cracked up when he heard how many knockouts I'd had: 'Doesn't surprise me with that temper of yours, boy,' he growled.

'Nah, I've learned to control it, Ron,' I answered. 'Honestly, I'm being a good lad now. I ain't got in no aggro, I promise you. I want to turn me life around. I know I can do it.'

Ron could tell by the earnest way I was talking that I was genuine. He saw the good in me, and I hoped he could advise me. After all, his own kids were doing well – his boy, Gary, was a copper – and he still is – and his daughter, Tracy, was married to one. I might have guessed what he was going to suggest. Why didn't I join the force too?

'I can't do that!' I said. 'All the training and then two years on the beat, walking around, looking like a biro refill.'

Everyone had to start somewhere, Ron pointed out, but I knew it wasn't for me. For one thing, I was associating with a lot of villains at the time.

Then Ron suggested the military. I was doubtful at first.

'Well, you should try!' he said. 'And there's only one regiment to be in, boy, and that's the Royal Marines. And don't you *ever* say Marines – that's the Americans. *Royal* Marines is here.' There was a recruiting station in Bermondsey for the reserves, which I could try out, but still I wasn't convinced.

I returned to the life of a fighter, but it wasn't the same. Deep down, I knew I needed to get myself together. Lee was doing well by then and he had a flat in Brixton and still worked in the scrap-yard, so I went to stay with him.

I filled out the recruitment form for the Royal Marines and forgot all about it. When I didn't hear anything, I guessed that I'd been rejected. But I was doing okay at the scrap-yard and I was due to take my driving test – finally! After all the years I'd spent on the road as an illegal.

And you know what? The test wasn't even that hard. I was delighted. And that wasn't the end of the good news.

The very next day I got a letter from the recruiters. I'd forgotten all about them! I had an interview at Bermondsey – and I sailed through. Later I found out that they had such a shortage of applicants that they were willing to take a risk on someone like me, who was a bit tasty. They'd seen my boxing history, too.

Even for someone like me, the training was gruelling and there were times, on 12-mile hikes with a 140-pound knapsack on my back, when I wondered if I'd make it, not least because we had to complete the course within a certain time or go back to the start. Somehow I got through it all and I was stationed at Northampton, home of the 7th Royal Anglian Heavy Artillery.

I soon realised I had a talent for marksmanship when I started getting top marks across the board for firing the machine gun – the same bit of kit that would get me in such trouble. For a while, though, the discipline of army life was just what I needed. I knew that I might die in battle, but if I did so, then it would be with dignity and honour, not alone in some gutter in Brixton. *This is going to be you now.* I had found a skill, something I was good at.

I had never bothered at school and yet now I found myself working all the time and paying close attention to every word the instructors said. It was completely different. I remembered the teachers who never seemed to be on my side and thought about how I'd never known I might actually achieve something if I studied.

It wasn't long before the Sniper Unit became interested in me, and they only wanted the best. It meant I would be with a new set of people – snipers operated separately; they had to. They needed to be ready to take out anyone, even if that person was a rogue soldier on the British side.

And then came Socket the sergeant, the river, the machine gun and the loss of my temper, which resulted in me being booted out of the Forces. For a while I felt really low. I didn't know how I was going to succeed at anything, but I was determined to try; I wasn't going to quit.

My friend Andy worked the doors at a club night in a Brixton pub and he invited me down to have a go. There was no licensing system so if my face fitted, I would be in. I got out a decent overcoat and went down there one Friday. It was an average night, with a couple of drunken Muppets who had to be slung out, but nothing too tricky. The Guv'nor told Andy he could see I was a bit tasty.

'Oh, yeah, fuck me, he's just been slung out of the Army for bashing a bleedin' NCO!' Andy told him.

The Guv'nor asked what regiment I'd been in and it turned out he'd also served in the Royal Marines. He wanted to know what had happened and whether I regretted it.

'Please don't ask me that,' I said, 'because I could kick meself up the arse! I'm gutted.'

'Well, I think you might have found your vocation,' he said. He had quite a few similar venues and suggested that I get a few guys together and handle the doors. Immediately I thought of asking my brothers Steve, Phillip and Lee – they were big boys and all quite handy; we'd laugh together at what we got up to. Steve did a factory once, broke in and nicked a load of stuff in bags, then got them back to Phil's house. He opened one bag and all he found was a load of old fashioned shirts, so he ripped open the other – and found the collars. We might not always be brilliant, but we knew we could count on each other.

Very quickly we gained a reputation for being a tight family, running most of the Guv'nor's pubs in Brixton and Streatham. With our smart suits, we looked the part, but more to the point, everyone knew you didn't mess with us. We didn't give a fuck – if you started in a pub run by the Snells, we'd smack you all over the gaff.

We soon got to know local faces like the Driscoll brothers and the Penfolds, notorious villains in their own right. But if they tried something, they got treated just the same as everyone else. We'd have a word, we'd just tell them not to start their bollocks – we didn't care who they were or who they thought they were, it wasn't going to happen in our pubs. Or if it did, we'd all go together. We'd just say that if they wanted a drink without getting damaged, they'd do as they were told and they'd play by the rules. Nine times out of ten, each one would be sweet as a nut. We actually became fairly friendly with the other families and they were quite a laugh. From my point of

Above left: My late grandfather, James Snelling – City of London Police Sergeant. He always wanted to stay on the beat.

Above right: My late Uncle Ron, former Scotland Yard detective.

Below: My late Grandmother, Doris Kathleen Snelling – the ambitious one. She was an Inspector in the City of London Police and went on to become Harold McMillan's Secretary – that's what we're led to believe.

Above: Me with my late father, James Alexander Snelling and my darling mum, celebrating Dad's 60th birthday (like the motor!).

Below: My brothers and sisters: Lee, Theresa, Alana, Melanie, Roy & Cliff. Sadly two brothers are not there – Steven passed away and Phil emigrated to Austrialia.

Above left: My cousin Gary – Traffic Division, Dorset. When he leaves he wants to join the circus – ha ha! He's retiring soon; good luck to him.

Above right: My dad, just a few weeks before he passed away.

Below: Me and the great Henry Cooper at a water rats do in 1985.

SECOND

FORM 19.

Additional Entries or Alterations in this Licence only to be made by an Official at the Head Office.

Name ....Roy Snell....

Address....152 Rosendale Road

....Dulwich....

....London SE21....

Licence No. 101174

Nationality ....British....

Renewal Fee Due

1st April 1985

Sig. ....Rudy....

Registration No. ....S 4631....

This Licence does not entitle the holder to enter any Tournament free of charge.

Above: Me and my trainer Greg Steene, this was taken at the Thomas A Beckett Gym in the Old Kent Road (handsome fighter, wasn't I).

Below: My official licence from the British Boxing Board of Control (what do you think of that tie?!)

Above: Going to collect monies owed (still look smart, don't I!)

Below: Me and my Victoria. I love this picture; we were in Spain.

Above left: Me with Gail Porter. She is such a lovely lady; it was a pleasure looking after her.

Above right: Me and David Ginola at the Oxford Union.

Below left: The lovely Barbara Windsor – such a great lady. I went on to work with her on *EastEnders* in 2000.

Below right: Eamonn Holmes. Used to wind him up all the time; he is so down to earth is Eamonn.

Above: Bodyguarding the legend Meat Loaf – a great man, a great artist.

Below: On set in 2000 working on *EastEnders*; it was a great experience.

TRAVEL...CONTINUED...

Tuesday 17th CONT.	ROY SNELL / RON KILLICK 7.55am Depart London Heathrow BA 456 11.20am Arrives Madrid
Friday 20th	GARTH CONDIT / FRANCESCA TOLOT / ROBERT VETECA / ROY SNELL / RON KILLICK 12.50pm Depart Madrid AF 1301 2.55pm Arrive Paris FAITH HILL / SAMUEL (TIM) McGRAW / GRACIE & MAGGIE McGRAW / DONNA WALDEN / CAROL FLY / JAMES JOHNSON / SANDRA WESTERMAN / ROY SNELL 10.00am Private jet flies Madrid Torrejon to Paris Le Bourget Flight time: 1 hour 35 mins, arrive 11.35pm
Saturday 21st	GARTH CONDIT / FRANCESCA TOLOT / ROBERT VETECA / ROY SNELL / RON KILLICK 9.00pm Depart Paris CDG AZ 331 11.00pm Arrive Rome
Sunday 22nd	FAITH HILL / SAMUEL (TIM) McGRAW / GRACIE & MAGGIE McGRAW / DONNA WALDEN / CAROL FLY / JAMES JOHNSON / SANDRA WESTERMAN / ROY SNELL Private jet flies Paris Le Bourget to Rome Ciampino Flight time: 1 hour 40 mins
Monday 23rd	FRANCESCA TOLOT / ROBERT VETECA / ROY SNELL / RON KILLICK 11.50am Depart Rome BA 553 1.30pm Arrive London FRANCESCA TOLOT / ROBERT VETECA 3.00pm Depart London BA 269 6.05pm Arrive Los Angeles GARTH CONDIT 12.10pm Depart Rome Delta 149 3.40pm Arrive New York JFK WESTERMAN 1.15pm Depart Rome AA111 4.35pm Arrive Chicago O'Hare 6.45pm Depart Chicago AA 1451 8.16pm Arrive New York

A bodyguard's life is such a glamorous life – you don't have to do much, do you!

view, what they did for a living was no business of mine, but I knew I wasn't going to go down that route.

Their life might look attractive to some, but only if you were prepared to take the consequences and that didn't interest me – I'd seen the headlines about what happened when they were crossed. The news was all about the mayhem they caused and how many people they smashed up, but you never heard what their victims had done to provoke them. I had little sympathy – I knew people wanted to play on their turf and take a little bit away for themselves; the real villains always find out.

And then what do they do? Come around to your house and say, 'You naughty boy, don't do it again?' They would smash you to a pulp – their justice, their way. Steal from them and they'd cut your fingers off.

My rule was: never cross the line, don't try to be smarter.

Villains have their rules and regulations, and me and my brothers never got involved in their business, but it was a two-way thing. In return the local families had to acknowledge that when they stepped through the doors they were in our manor. Our rules. Don't take the piss or we dealt with it our way, and our way was sometimes quite painful.

We heard a nightclub in Herne Hill called the Bon Bonne was opening and the owner, Colin Lockett, wanted to discuss security. I went down to see the place. Talk about exclusive – he'd spent a million pounds on the interiors alone! I went down to speak to Colin and his brother Barry, and although we didn't come cheap, they took us on. We did that club for years.

It took a while for the club to take off, but it became our flagship after we dissuaded the shit from trying to get in – the cardboard gangsters. They'd come down in their P-reg

Jaguars, suits and £15 in their pockets; they thought they were proper faces. They'd always be trying to make out they knew some big man or other – 'Come on, Roysie, you must know Frank the Plank' – but it was all nonsense and we'd just sling them out. They were nothing compared to the real gangsters.

And I should know. I did some work for a genuine Mr Big – and that's all I'll call him. This wasn't another plastic wannabe – even *my* arse went a bit. He laughed when he saw he had my full attention. I still didn't want to get involved in anything dodgy, but it turned out he only wanted someone to collect cash from his pubs of a night. He revealed that he couldn't trust his own people. I guessed it was a test to see if he could get me to do less legal stuff for him, but what did I care? It was just a bit of graft.

I ended up going from one end of the Old Kent Road to the other – he owned every fucking pub and club along it! To help me, I took along my mate Dean Smith, an ex-bare knuckle fighter, a smashing bloke, I loved him like a brother – still do.

We'd come out of some pubs with fourteen grand in a Tesco's carrier bag and take it all back to Mr Big. Casually, he'd pull a big handful of notes out of one of the bags and pass it over to me as payment for the evening's work. Without counting, I pocketed it and gave Dean a cut outside. Even then I'd still have hundreds left over: it was a good job.

One night Mr Big asked me for some advice. He'd been approached by a film company, who wanted to do a movie loosely based around his life: his part was to be played by an actor by the name of Bob Hoskins. They wanted to use Mr Big's own boat for a scene. I thought he was going on about some little river cruiser, but then he took me to see it.

It was a 50-berth yacht on the Thames, the whole business. En-suite bathrooms, kitchens... It must have been a million pounds' worth of boat and the movie people were going to pay him twenty grand just to borrow it. Where I came in was to sort out all the details for kitting it out and filming, but it went very smoothly. And if you see *The Long Good Friday*, that bit with the boat on the Thames – that's the actual yacht.

I wasn't quite at the stage where I could think about getting my own yacht, not quite yet, but I was about to take a step up. I'd been working hard and maintaining my reputation for being trustworthy and honest. Off the back of that, I got a call to be head of security at the Lyceum in the Strand, where hot acts on the way to stardom would play showcase sets for their fans and music-industry bigwigs.

I had an interview with a fella called Ron Weston at the Lyceum headquarters. He was a bit late and so I popped out and got a sandwich and a cup of tea, before settling back to wait. I'd just got comfortable when the door opened and he appeared. I thought, *Fuck me, I know that geezer from somewhere!* We looked each other over and then I saw that he recognised me too. I just couldn't remember where we knew each other from, but he could.

'You beat me up five years ago,' he told me. 'I'm the guy you knocked out in the second round.' He'd been one of the fighters that I'd taken on in my amateur career – and he'd lasted longer than most. I'd given him a punch that I called my 'Night Nurse' – sent him straight to sleep. But here he was, running the Lyceum in London. He'd gone all the way to the top of the pole.

'You've done well for yourself, boy, ain't you?' I said. It was a bit of a bonus to know my future boss and even if the circumstances had been a bit unusual, it established a sort of bond between us from the start. He knew I could take care of myself and that I'd be professional; the Lyceum would be safe with me in it.

Eager for me to start as soon as possible, he signed me up and I had to go back to Brixton and let Mr Big know that I wouldn't be able to collect his money for him after the weekend. He was clearly disappointed and hoped that my brothers might be interested in taking over, but there was no way they would leave the club and so I prepared for my last Saturday working for him.

That evening one of his other lads, Big Bill, came up to me and growled, 'Oi, Roysie, I hear you're going.' I told him it was true.

'You know what, the boss ain't half gutted,' he said.

'What do you mean?'

'Oh, he had plans for you. Big plans. I think you're a fool to leave, mate, I really do. I mean, what are you going to earn at the Lyceum? Tuppence! Mickey Mouse fucking bands, all that shit! You could earn a fortune – he'd look after you well. He's done you proud.'

'Oi,' I said, 'Excuse me. Whatever I've earned, I've deserved it.' I asked him what he meant by 'big plans'.

'Well, you know, I can't say too much,' he muttered. 'You know who the man is. I ain't gotta tell you, have I?'

But I knew what he meant. I'd been right all along – Mr Big wanted me to get fully involved in his world.

It went against everything I believed in.

'Listen,' I told Bill, 'no matter what big plans he may *think* he had for me, I can tell you now the answer would have been, "no," 'cos as soon as he asked me to go down that route, I'd have been gone. I'm doing what I always wanted to do. To you it might have been tuppence, to me it's an honest living.'

But I knew what would have been in store for me and I'd made the right decision to move on. Me and Mr Big ended on a good note when I was able to tell him that Deanie had decided to stay on and was going to keep his brother Lee with him, too.

Mr Big still wanted me to stay. As a mark of respect, he got all his men to leave us alone before confiding in me that if anything went wrong in my new job, I could always come back.

'My grandfather and uncle were on the straight and narrow,' I said. 'I could easily have gone down the wrong way – you know my history. But I always knew that I would turn out the right way. I will not put my father to shame by becoming something I don't wish to be, but I don't hold a grudge against anyone else for what they do – it's entirely up to them.'

He could see that I meant it.

'Yeah, I know,' he said. 'But I want to say thanks from the bottom of my heart, mate. It's very rare I trust anyone, but you I trust like my own son.'

He told me he had a little something for me and gave me a bag as I left. I was touched – he didn't need to do that. Leaving the office for the last time, I got in my car without looking in the bag – by then I had a 4.2 Jag, I liked my cars – until I got back to my flat and spilled out the contents on the bed – it was a nice bit of cash.

It was time to start my new life.

CHAPTER 4

THE LYCEUM

He was one of the most powerful Yardies in Britain and I needed his help. His name was Tanamo and I wasn't likely to forget it – not least because he had it spelt out in diamonds set in his teeth; he didn't really do casual. His regular outfit included vast amounts of bling, but I didn't let the flashy appearance fool me. He listened carefully to what I had to say. At heart, Tanamo was just a Brixton businessman. I might not agree with the sort of business he did, but I reckoned he would give my straightforward proposition a fair hearing. And I was in trouble, if he didn't.

'Here are ten tickets for you and your family to see LL Cool J and Public Enemy at the Brixton Academy,' I told him. 'I'd like you to come backstage before the gig and meet the bands.' I could tell I'd won him over, but I hadn't finished yet. 'The night's going to be on me. Take them out for a nice meal then come to the show, enjoy yourselves.' With that, I handed over a few quid.

I'd shown him the utmost respect. And in return, I added, I wanted a few of his boys outside the venue so that we could ensure the artists would be able to get from the tour bus into the venue.

I was the only white face doing security for the US rappers, but my family was well known in south London and my reputation preceded me – that was why the Brixton Academy lads had asked me to head up the team in the first place. Tanamo didn't even need to think twice about my request.

'Leave it to me, man,' he drawled. 'Me know what you say, Rahysie. Me get you in and out the building quickly enough. I'll make it all right.'

He wasn't joking.

Tanamo's boys formed an impenetrable guard of honour from the tour bus to the stage door – at least 50 yards – and all the way down the corridor and into the dressing room – another 50 yards. Each was dressed exactly the same: black from head-to-toe with matching sunglasses. One look at them and you could tell there wouldn't be any trouble. They looked *awesome*. The US artists were absolutely stunned.

And they were nice boys and loved the reception I'd arranged for them. That guy with the big clock from Public Enemy – Flavor Flav – he was a smashing fella. 'Hey, Roysie,' he said with a grin when he saw the arrangements. 'Man, you're bad-ass!' It cracked him up. 'Man, I wouldn't get in your way.'

Tanamo was waiting for us in the dressing room with his family.

'You like my boys, Roysie? You like them?' he said.

At last I felt relaxed enough to give him a big smile: 'You've done me proud, Tan, you've done all right, son.'

One last touch: I asked Flavor Flav to namecheck Tanamo on stage and he did it in great style, roaring, 'The man's here! The main fucking man in Brixton, man! Come to see us. Tanamo's here, take a bow, man.'

Of course, Tanamo thought he was fucking king as he got up to acknowledge the massive cheer from the packed audience. It was an incredible gig, such a great atmosphere.

And it absolutely made me in Brixton.

I could do no wrong and suddenly my entire family was the safest in the area. My sisters could walk down Brixton Hill at 3am covered in jewellery and nobody would touch them. Everyone knew who their brother was.

For the next six nights straight, Tanamo put on the same level of security and the rappers were so impressed with what I'd organised that they asked me to go on tour with them. That was the first time I realised that I could really make a proper go of the bodyguarding, that I might be really good at it.

My main gig was at the Lyceum Theatre in the West End of London. My brother Phil had taken over the Bon Bonne for me and my brother Cliffy came with me.

It was a great time to be starting out in music: the early 1980s – all those trendy bands, with their weird names! The first act I looked after was A-ha and that was just the start – Duran Duran, Wham!, Depeche Mode... They were all coming up and they all sounded pretty unlikely. Some of them had just got started, like A-ha – whose first showcase sold so badly, it was cancelled – and others, like Wham!, had been going for months and enjoyed a few hits. I've seen all those eighties' revival shows like *Here and Now* and I laughed when I realised I'd worked with every single one of the bands first time around – Haircut 100, Spandau Ballet, Nick Heyward... Tell you what – they all look like they've lived a bit since then!

At the Lyceum, I was in charge of every aspect of

security, from the moment the artist stepped out of their vehicle into the building. Backstage... onstage... I was with them every step of the way. I'd stay close to make sure they weren't bothered by any of the fans while they were performing. Throughout the venue, I positioned the rest of my team – in the auditorium, backstage, front of house, you name it. Each of them had radios and we were in contact all the time.

Bodyguarding was a mystery to me back then; that was a different world. Close protection, they called it. The bodyguards – or 'close protection officers' as they liked to call themselves – worked under the personal direction of the tour managers, delivering and collecting the artist. Even then I could feel the lure of that life. That was what I really wanted to do.

As a bodyguard, you had to think on your feet. You needed to be able to develop new and better ways of protecting the client – you've got to use your brain more than your fists. Just a few seconds might make all the difference. It wasn't a game for those who just want a bit of a row.

I got to see those bodyguards at work as I took artists from the stage door through to hospitality – the green room. One glam star arrived already in his gear, giving it large to everyone and swaggering along with a couple of his own minders, the best in the business. He was a huge star. Rather than just take him to the stage door, they would accompany him all the way to the stage and keep an eye on him throughout his performance.

But his band was left to wander in on their own. The singer was already in the green room with water, fruit and a special little steam bath for his throat to loosen up his vocal cords in the warm-up before they all went on stage.

All the while I was in the background, observing, watching how smoothly they worked, where they stood on the wings of the stage and just making little mental notes of how they did things. I was interested to see that both stood to the back of the stage, whereas I would lurk behind the curtain at the front so that if anyone tried to get on stage, I'd be able to grab them immediately.

The gig went really well and the crowd was absolutely mad for the flamboyant showman. He was pulling all the moves and strutting about like a peacock; the atmosphere was terrific. But I was still wondering about that onstage bodyguard formation and when at last the final encore was played and the sweaty performers gave their last salute to the crowd and returned to the safety of the dressing room, I went up to the bigger bodyguard, a black guy called Neil, and asked him about where they were standing.

'Oh, you noticed that, did you?' asked Neil.

'Yeah, just curious.'

'I just got the biggest bollocking of my life,' he admitted, pointing out the other guy, Greg, who was the Guv'nor. 'I've only been doing it four weeks and I assumed I had to stand away from them.'

But Greg had overheard our conversation and came up to me.

'Fuck me! You're a bit clued-up, aren't you? Good job you were standing where Neil was supposed to be.'

Right there and then he asked me to join his team. Whenever his firm happened to bring artists to the Lyceum, he said, I could look after them. I could see how that might work and Cliffy would deputise for me in the venue.

And that's where it started. I had entered the world of the close protection bodyguard, it was that casual. No licensing requirements – just Greg, what he'd learned over his career and a bunch of his lads. I had scope to develop my own techniques. And if I was smart, I could do well.

The first thing I learned was D-bus and E-bus (Delivery and Exit, when it wasn't referred to as Long Reach and Short Reach). I watched what everyone else did and soon evolved my own methods. By the time they got to us, some of the other fellas had been travelling the world with the acts for eight or nine months and they were very smooth. One bodyguard would go to the left, one to the right of the client and then there'd be one in the middle in front and they would close in and then walk them in. It was a very tight little triangle formation. *Christ! You couldn't get to them if you tried: they had every angle covered.*

When I got to do it, I always took the left-hand flank – in other words, standing to the left of the client. That was always the position I played throughout my career, even when I started my own company. That was where I felt comfortable, where I was tight.

I knew I could hit anyone with a Night Nurse from the left, my strongest punch. If someone ever managed to get through from the other side, I still had a pretty tasty right.

It wasn't long before I was working with a dizzying array of stars. I looked the part, too: smart Armani suits, spiky hair and my goatee – well, it *was* the 1980s! The Lyceum was always busy and when it wasn't doing bands, high-profile music biz events were hosted there and so I got a broad range of experience, which would be very useful years later when I set up my own firm.

The first of the bands that Greg worked with was Spandau Ballet, led by the Kemp brothers. I rode with them in the tour bus from the hotel to the venue. *At last I was doing what I'd only watched before.* Then I walked them to their dressing room, got them on stage, made sure they were safe and got them off again and into their tour bus. They did three nights and it all went so well.

The Lyceum's Ron Weston got to hear about my new responsibilities and he passed me acts that didn't have their own bodyguards. I've always been one to jump in at the deep end and so I just got stuck in. As before, Cliff took over my job and I did the bodyguarding. My first experience of doing it for the Lyceum was with Kajagoogoo – *what was with those names? Kaja-bloody-googoo!* But they were really pleased with how that went.

Duran Duran was quite an operation: they were there for a full five nights and I had to stay with them all day. It was a big moment for my brother too because suddenly he was totally in charge of the venue while I had to spend all my time with the band. They were staying at the Hyde Park Hotel.

I was totally in Greg's world, away from the familiar surroundings of the Strand and entirely responsible for the safety of one of the UK's most exciting acts. If anything happened to them, there would be a lot of heartbroken young ladies who'd be after revenge! You needed a cool head. Greg threw mock scenarios at me. I'm not often lost for words and on that occasion, I didn't even need to pause for breath. Everything just came to me – what to look out for, where to stand, how to make sure that the boys were safe... I was pretty confident. Greg looked pleased with my suggestions.

He told me to work with Neil, the fella I'd talked to at the glam-rock gig, and put my plans into action that night for Duran Duran. In the meantime, Greg said, he would take a back seat and just watch how I did it all. As always, I just got on with the job and didn't worry too much about whether I'd got it right. I was pretty good at what I did and I wasn't one to get anxious about decisions: I knew that if I just did it sensibly, then it should work out okay.

The gig went really well and the band put in a great performance. We got them back on the bus okay, tired but elated at a good start to the week. We all got along really well. I thought it was important to build a good rapport with the artists, not just stand there scowling, like an angry piece of meat. You want to have a chat with them, put them at their ease and make it seem like fun.

It was part of my role to get them back to the hotel and to stay there, then repeat the whole process every day for the rest of the week. But first, I needed to hear what Greg had to say about doing it the Roysie way. But I didn't have long to wait – and he didn't have much to say.

'As from now,' said Greg to the entire team, while he pointed over one shoulder at me, 'this guy's in charge. Listen to what he says, watch what he does, because I'm telling you now, he's going to go far. I've seen some guys in my time, but Roy takes the biscuit!'

By the end of the week it was pretty clear that there would be a position for me in Greg's firm if I wanted it. Spandau Ballet was going on a European tour and I could have gone with them, if only I'd said the word.

To be honest, I just wasn't interested. My head wasn't turned by that sort of thing: I was happy doing a bit of both jobs, head of security and close protection, and that's the way it was going to stay. I'd never been abroad and I didn't even have a passport. So it was that a mate on the firm, Steve Smart, took the tour and I went back to the Lyceum. There was enough going on there to keep me very busy.

I couldn't quite believe it when I heard that a band was

coming to do seven nights. A few did five nights, like Duran Duran, but seven was unheard of. And the manager of the Lyceum couldn't even tell me who it was. All he knew was they had a girl singer and they'd had a single that went to No. 4, with the latest one at No. 2. With any luck, it might reach No. 1 by the Sunday; that was all we knew.

That Monday, what we called the 'gigster' turned up with all the speakers and the microphones and the roadies. It was a whirlwind as they set up, soundchecked and generally readied themselves for the night's performance. I was chatting to a couple of the roadies when my attention wandered to a vision floating through the stage door. It was this bird wearing a tutu, ballerina shoes and her short hair sticking up in the air. She looked an absolute sight! And she had this big thick line of bright make-up going straight across the middle of her face: eyes, nose, the lot.

''Ello,' I muttered. 'What the hell is *that*?'

But the roadie looked round and then stopped me before I could say anything else.

'She's the lead singer!' he hissed.

'You're kidding me, ain'tcha?' I said, adding sarcastically, 'She's going to go far, looking like that. State of her!'

And then a geezer came in wearing a suit covered in flower patterns. I thought, *have a look at these!*

Cliffy came down to join us and he went, ''Oo the hell's that?' We reckoned this pair had absolutely no chance. But when the woman came up to us, she was extremely well-spoken with an attractive Scottish accent.

'How are you?' she said to me dreamily. 'You have lovely eyes.'

'Sorry?' I said.

'You have lovely eyes,' she repeated.

''Ave I? Thanks very much, luv. The green room's just along here.'

I got rid of her just as the rest of the band came in – and they looked much less weird. I felt a bit sorry for them, tied up with those two odd characters.

The Lyceum's manager turned up and by then, he knew who the band was.

'They've got a very strange name,' he remarked.

'You should see them in person! They look even weirder,' was my reply.

'Yes, I don't think the name's very catchy. They're called Eurythmics.'

How wrong we were!

And once you got to know Annie Lennox and Dave Stewart, they were absolutely smashing. A former schoolteacher, she was very down-to-earth, really lovely. And even back then, that first night I heard them, her voice was incredible. We all got on so well and even she had a bit of a tear in her eye when it came to go. She gave me a big hug and a kiss, and then said, 'You know, I wasn't sure when I first met you, because you didn't seem to like us.'

'I did think you was a bit of a freak,' I admitted with my usual honesty. But once she'd come offstage and got changed, she was quite a normal girl – quite a looker, too, once she'd got all that crap off her face. I wished her all the best, but she hardly needed it. She and Dave Stewart went on to sell more than 25 million records.

We did the Rock and Pop Awards every year, which later became the Brit Awards. All the bands I worked with were up for some gong or other – Wham!, Duran Duran and the rest. Pepsi and Shirlie were Wham!'s backing singers at the time. Many years later I was working with Martin Kemp on *EastEnders* and he told me he was married.

I asked if his missus was in the same game as him. He said she wasn't, but she used to be a singer with Wham!. It only turned out to be Shirlie! He insisted I come in and meet her again and even though it had been 15 years since I'd last seen her, she came out, took one look and went, 'Oh my gawd! It's you!'

''Allo, sweetheart,' I said, 'Nice to see you after all this time.' Even though I'd worked with so many artists over the years, it was good when we still remembered one another.

Not every act I worked with was successful. Spider thought it would be a great idea to throw these pyrotechnics called thunder flashes into the crowd. The manager of the Lyceum was entirely unimpressed by their antics. He called down over the radio that he wanted them out. At first I thought I'd misheard him – how was I supposed to get rid of an act when there were 3,000 screaming fans watching them go mad?

'I don't care,' he told me. 'I don't want them in my theatre. Get them out now!'

So I had no choice: I got a couple of my lads and we went mob-handed onstage in front of the whole crowd and physically pulled the band off, then slung them out the stage door.

Following this, we chucked their equipment out after them – drums, microphones, speakers and all. That wasn't my proudest moment. But the papers loved it. The next day the tabloids were full of it – Band Gets Ejected By Own Bouncers, all that kind of stuff. I never heard of Spider again.

Then there was Notoriety. *Christ, this lot are going to be a nightmare!* I thought. They looked like a bad dream for a start, and they had on these awful horror masks. Then the lead singer got out an aerosol can, held a lighter under the nozzle and sprayed flames over the heads of the crowd. He did it in such a way that it looked like fire was coming out of his mouth.

Didn't matter what it looked like – I knew what would happen next and, sure enough, my earpiece crackled into life and I was told to go on stage mid-song and get them to stop. I hated doing that.

'S'cuse me, old chap, would you mind not flame-throwing the crowd?'

I guess it couldn't always be rock'n'roll.

CHAPTER 5

REGGIE AND RON'S NIECE

The Colonel was a boxing promoter who staged contests at the Lyceum. Of course, the fighting game has always had its connections with the Underworld and the Colonel was well respected. The Richardsons, Roy Shaw, Freddie Foreman, Joey Pyle and Lenny Mclean all wanted to talk with him and shake him by the hand.

I was doing the security for the Colonel's second match at the Lyceum when my eye was caught by the ring-girl – she who paraded around with the display board before each round. She was a real looker: blonde hair and blue eyes. Her name was Stacey and I barely even noticed Greg coming down the corridor as we chatted in a break.

'Cor, you two will be lovers next,' he joked, as he passed by.

Back at the ring, Stacey pointed out the Colonel to me.

'That's my uncle,' she said.

Typical. Putting my big foot in it! The Colonel hardly knew me and there I was, picking up his niece.

And the Kray brothers were Stacey's other uncles or at least they said that they were; I didn't think they had any nieces. And she wasn't a blood relation. But they knew the Colonel and that was good enough.

Stacey and I started seeing each other that very night, although she didn't mention her other uncles to me for a while and I couldn't say I blamed her.

I was helping out in the Colonel's office when he was deep in conversation with a sharply dressed man that he called Charlie.

''Ow you settling in?' asked Charlie. 'You doing all right, son?'

'Yeah, yeah, I'm just cracking on,' I replied. We didn't talk long. I thought he seemed a nice enough fellow.

'Yeah, they're not all bad. Don't listen to everything you hear about the Krays,' said the Colonel later.

That was Charlie Kray? I hadn't even known I was meeting him and already I was dating his niece. It was enough to make even me break out in a light sweat.

It wasn't long after that when the Colonel announced he was going to Broadmoor and he wanted me to drive him. I hadn't got a clue where it was, but he was a regular visitor and so he knew the way. He specifically wanted me to come down because there was a patient who wanted to meet me.

That night, I was staying at Stacey's and she told me that a letter had come for me that day. The writing on the envelope was very strange – I could barely make out what it said. It was like a child had scribbled on it, but I ripped it open and inside, the letter said only:

> *Looking forward to meeting you tomorrow,*
> *so we can chat about Stacey.*
>
> *Ron*

Fucking hell! In less than a day I would be meeting one of Stacey's *other* uncles.

At least we had a decent ride. The Colonel had just bought a brand new 2.8 Granada Ghia X – a lovely motor. Fully loaded; leather interior, air conditioning, tilting electric sunroof and a Sharp cassette-radio, which could do fast forward – and reverse. It was the nuts of a motor. Champagne gold. Beautiful – absolutely the car to be seen driving in.

But then we got to Broadmoor, just outside London. What a bloody place! You feel its brooding presence before you even get there. It housed some of the most dangerous characters in the country and it was billed as a 'hospital' rather than a prison. All I can say is, it felt bloody weird getting there.

The reception was in a massive hallway and the security as tight as you might imagine. You have to sign a book to get in and once you've done that, you're funnelled through to another similar area, where you do it all again. Eventually we got to the visiting room.

There must have been 50 or 60 people already there. The patients were about to be let in through the cell door at the far end of the room. While everyone waited, two blokes pushed around trolleys from which they served tea and cakes and biscuits. The Colonel and I sat down at a table. Then the door opened and in streamed all the patients.

Well, almost all. No sign of anyone for us.

Everyone was chatting as the minutes passed. It couldn't have been long that we were hanging about, but it didn't half drag when we were just sitting around.

The door through which the patients had emerged swung shut, but the Colonel didn't seem to be concerned.

'Don't worry, son. He's probably still getting ready.'

Getting ready? What for?

Then the door opened.

The figure stepping through was immaculate. I am talking a beautiful navy-blue Armani suit with a white shirt, a silk Bloom tie and very subtle jewellery – a discreet matching ring and bracelet. The man's hair was slicked back and he wore a pair of black-framed glasses. As he stepped into the room, everyone went silent. Every single patient stood up as one, quickly followed by all the visitors. A ripple of applause spread through the room, polite little taps on the heels of the palms and, as Ronnie Kray strode towards our table, he acknowledged the reception with a tight smile and a sharp wave of the hand. It was as if he were a movie star.

'Thank you, thank you very much,' he nodded.

It was an amazing sight to see.

I'd never seen such respect before – utmost respect. It must have reinforced Ronnie's image of himself as the number one man, which, of course, he was, but it was slightly surreal to think that his respect was coming from inmates of Britain's most secure psychiatric hospital.

He sat down with two packs of cigarettes and one already lit. I noticed straightaway that he sat to one side and turned his head every time he spoke. His voice was soft, an effect accentuated by the way he held his hand slightly in front of his mouth when he spoke. Ronnie was convinced that he was being monitored by lip-readers – even after all those years, he was still cautious.

While the two old friends chatted away – or in Ronnie's case, muttered out of the corner of his mouth – one of the trolley guys reached our table. 'Would you like tea or coffee?' he asked. I looked up and realised it was another patient.

I'm not drinking anything served by this lot! I wasn't even going to have a biscuit.

The Colonel saw my horrified face and kicked me under the table as if to warn, 'Behave your bleedin' self!' But it wasn't just nerves. I was sure that I recognised the bloke from somewhere. Surely not! I dismissed the notion. This was Broadmoor. From where would I know one of the patients? My thoughts were interrupted as Ronnie addressed me.

'How ya getting on?' he hissed. 'I hear you're seeing my niece. I hope you treat her with respect.'

'Of course, Mr Kray, without a shadow of a doubt – I'm not stupid!'

'I like that,' he said. 'You hold your own.' He was used to yes-men and my cheeky attitude was refreshing. 'You're not impressed by any of this, are you?' he said, gesturing at all the visitors, who were staring at him with undisguised admiration.

I said, 'Not really, no.'

He went back to Stacey. 'Have you put a ring on her finger yet?'

'No,' I admitted, 'but give me half a chance – it's only been seven months.' I was only partly joking. I didn't really know exactly how I felt about her at that point, but Ronnie must have picked up on something because within three months me and Stacey were engaged.

I'm not sure what Ronnie had thought I would be like before that first meeting, but I think he approved of me. As well as our chat had gone, I was still only too relieved to get out of that place and away from its brooding atmosphere. It wasn't until we were in the car and speeding back to London that I realised how stressful the whole thing had been.

The Colonel was more used to it, being an old friend of Ronnie's, and over time I would become accustomed to the drive down as my role developed into being his informal minder. There was never any trouble around the Colonel, but he was just one of those guys who liked to have the authority that came with the presence of someone who looked as if they could half handle themselves. And I felt very protective towards him. I became very close to him and his family, and he in turn took a keen interest in me, investing time and effort in teaching me a great deal about how to make a go of business and how to handle myself without resorting to fists.

I next saw Ronnie the following Wednesday. As a regular, the Colonel was allowed to sit where we had been before, but I wasn't permitted to visit the same person two weeks running and so I was assigned to another patient at an adjoining table. The Colonel had sorted it all out.

'You'll be there, mate. He's a nice bloke – I think you'll like him,' he told me. 'Just speak to him like you'd speak to anyone else. He deserves it – he doesn't get a lot of visitors.' My visitor turned out to be the trolley-pusher I'd been so suspicious of the week before.

Ronnie's entrance was just as theatrical as before – the big build-up, the immaculate suit, the standing ovation from the other patients and their visitors. I nodded and smiled a hello as he sat down. He looked away to the Colonel without acknowledging me.

''Oo's that?' he demanded, gesturing at me.

Momentarily startled, I was about to tell him he'd met me just six days earlier when the Colonel managed to turn and kick me under the table without Ronnie seeming to notice.

Don't question him.

The Colonel answered, 'That's Roy, Ronnie. He's the one who's seeing Stacey.'

Ronnie and me had exactly the same conversation as the week before.

'I hope you're going to treat her all right, son.'

'Don't worry, Ronnie...' Word for word, and he never once remembered that he'd met me. Poor bloke, I felt quite sorry for him, but I was also relieved to turn away to talk to the patient to whom I'd been assigned, though it was quickly apparent that he wasn't interested in small talk.

'I know you,' he said, flatly.

A strange day was getting stranger. And yet... once I came to look at him properly, I realised that he was right.

'My name's Charlie Smith,' he said.

And then it came back to me: Ashford Young Prison. He had been in the adult side of the prison and he was the one that the screws got to talk to me in an effort to scare me out of my life of crime. He was the one who'd been an axe murderer. I couldn't help but reflect that now I was sitting opposite him with nothing between us except an ordinary table.

What was it he'd said at Ashford? 'I can't wait to meet you this side. We'll see how hard you are then.' But now he looked perfectly normal – as the Colonel said, a perfectly nice fella. He explained that he'd been rather busy since we last met. After having been let out – I'm not sure if his sentence came to an end or if he'd managed to get some kind of day release – he killed the rest of the family that he'd first attacked.

'They done me up like a good 'un,' he said, 'so I thought, well, I had to do 'em.' There was no hint of emotion in his voice – we might have been discussing the weather. I realised there was no way that I could let him know the horror I felt.

'Not an axe again, surely?' I inquired, conversationally.

'Yeah,' he confirmed, 'I done 'em with the axe.'

'You don't half like an axe, you, don't you?' I said. 'What is it with you and axes?'

'Well, it's quick and clean, innit?' he said. Utterly calm throughout our conversation, his voice was never raised. *That's all there is to it. That's the way I deal with things.* There was no sense of right or wrong with him. Other than that, he was fine. I felt sorry for him for being such a sick man.

'I'm trying to become a songwriter,' he told me. Later, I heard that some of his numbers had been picked up and performed by well-known artists. He was just like any other aspiring singer, but at the same time I was still very glad when the Colonel finished talking with Ronnie, who again sat side-on, his hand cupped over his mouth as he muttered away.

It was only right that I should meet Stacey's other 'uncle'. Reggie Kray was being held at Parkhurst at the time and so we took a ferry over to the Isle of Wight to visit him some time after I'd become engaged to Stacey.

But the day didn't start well.

The Colonel lost his bracelet over the side of the boat – and this wasn't any old bracelet: his name had been set in it in diamonds. But he had plenty of time to cool off about it at the prison while we waited to see Reggie. We had to wait ages. When we finally got through all the checks, we were led into a room that contained only one inmate – Reggie Kray himself. Just one prison warder was standing at the back of the room, where Reggie sat to receive us. I shook his hand and the Colonel started to introduce us.

'Yeah – I know who he is,' interrupted Reggie. From the start, he seemed cold and unfriendly, but he was more direct than his twin – there was none of that whispering into his hand. We sat down and the screw behind him walked out without a word. No guards at all now, just the three of us. I couldn't help but glance around, but he was left all on his own.

'I hear you're going to be marrying my niece,' he said, with an arrogance in the way he spoke. Even though he was who he was, I didn't like it.

'Well, yeah,' I replied sharply. 'You got that right.'

'What are your plans, then?'

'I haven't got any at the moment.'

'Will you take care of her?'

'Of course I will. I wouldn't be marrying her otherwise, would I?'

For a bit, we went backwards and forwards and I don't think he liked me very much. The feeling was quite mutual, but later meetings went more smoothly. I think he ended up seeing that I wasn't such a bad fella. He liked the fact that I had balls and would stand up to him, even if the respect was grudging – I probably got about an eight out of ten from him. We were just dancing around each other, really. Eventually, I was always going to respect him – he and Ronnie were, after all, the Krays – I was never going to forget that.

I did it the proper way and asked Stacey's father, Peter, for her hand in marriage. The wedding took a lot of planning because she didn't want things done by halves. We were married in 1983.

In the early days of our marriage, we were so happy. I bought us a beautiful house in Dartford, in Kent, and our daughter Victoria was born. But the marriage never really stood a chance: we got together too young.

Wherever we went, Stacey would turn heads and she was always the centre of attention at parties. She thrived on it.

I'd be out working late and I remember coming back and crashing out on the sofa. When I woke up next morning, she was lying next to me and I realised that she'd come in even later than I had and she still had her make-up on. But when I asked her what she'd been up to, she'd say that she'd been up and had only just put it on.

It didn't add up and eventually I found out that she was having an affair with a Dartford fireman. I went to the fire station but the man in question had heard all about me and my reputation and decided he'd rather not come out in the street to discuss the situation. I couldn't say I blamed him, but that was the end of my marriage. Not long after that, we split up for good, but it's not something I like to dwell on and I don't want to go into too much detail. All I did was throw myself back into the graft and moved into London to be on my own.

Victoria stayed with her mum, who wouldn't let me see her for years, but I tried to remember her birthdays. When things got very bad for me and I had little dough, I had to walk all the way from London to their place in Kent – a journey of 12 miles. I only had enough money for a card with a tenner in the envelope and I set out with my present early in the morning. It wasn't the most pleasant stroll I've ever had and when I got to Dartford, I found that the letterbox was sealed. I banged on the door, but Stacey wouldn't open it. I couldn't even leave the card.

It wasn't until years later that I heard from Victoria again. I was in the Jag when a text message came through: 'I bet you thought this would never happen, but it has. Merry Christmas, love Victoria, your daughter.'

I hadn't seen her since she was three. I didn't know what to do. When I got home, I was in a right state.

What do I say after 15 years? What the hell do I say?

Victoria had seen a feature on me in a magazine. But it wasn't as if she knew me, she just happened to point out this big fella who did the special bodyguarding to her cousin.

'Hmm,' her cousin replied. 'That's yer father.'

'Oh, shut up! You're joking...'

'No, that *is* your dad.'

Like me, Stacey had remarried by then and Victoria had long thought of the new man as her dad, but after she saw that article she got on the Internet and tracked me down.

I phoned her back the same night.

'Hello,' I said.

'Hello?' she said.

'It's your father,' I said, then she burst into tears.

'I don't know what to say.'

'Nor do I. Let's meet for lunch – I'll pick you up on Friday.'

I got a lift to her work with a fellow bodyguard, who was going straight on to travel by private jet to Algiers. He was about to bodyguard a diplomat and Victoria came out of her work to see him with his bulletproof flak jacket already on and me standing on the opposite side of the car in my suit, overcoat and earpiece.

'Oh my God!' said Victoria. 'Mum was right.'

'What?'

'Are you a gangster?'

'No, I'm not a bloody gangster!'

I went on to explain that I had become an elite bodyguard and that I ran my own company. It wasn't like a regular job and my man had to be ready to start work straightaway from the moment he got off the plane. She listened to what we did and realised for the first time that Dad wasn't exactly what Mum said he was.

It was a bit of a breakthrough. After all those years apart, I knew that I was still on the outside – I always will be. But after a few false starts, she's stayed in contact with me.

We never got to share all those special times of growing up, not the way I have with Eden, my daughter from my second marriage, but me and Victoria have a relationship now. She's a woman now, a young lady. I am so sorry I wasn't there when she was a child – I really missed that bit.

CHAPTER 6

BONNIE'S SHOES

It was time for UB40 to go on stage, but as I opened their dressing room door, I was hit by a, shall we say, *pungent* smell. To make matters worse, there were no windows in there. They were lovely lads, very down-to-earth, but they only just about managed to clamber onto the stage and it hardly seemed as if they'd be able to play anything.

But the crowd swarmed to the front and started to nod away as the reggae beat kicked in and the band looked so laidback, I wouldn't have been surprised if they'd all slipped into a coma. I don't know if the fans guessed what their idols had been smoking backstage, but from where I was standing, it was fucking hilarious.

Most nights, Bert the manager used to come down just to check that everything was okay. That night, he turned up just as I was heading off the stage and through the arch in the corridor that led to the dressing room. You could still smell the same distinct odour, even before you entered the room. Bert, bless him, wasn't exactly a man of the world, but even he noticed that something was going on.

''Allo, Roy,' he began. '*Cor!* My goodness, that's a bad

smell! Do you think we need to get someone in to check the drains?' He was such an innocent and I was forced to control an urge to burst out laughing, but to be honest, he was better off not knowing and I seized on the opportunity he'd presented me to get out of having to cover up for the band.

'Nah,' I said, straight-faced. 'I think it'll be fine, mate. Knowing that lot, they probably had a Ruby Murray.' And I just left it at that and he walked off, completely satisfied and oblivious to what had really been going on.

The band, meanwhile, were having a fantastic time on stage. They simply brought the house down. I knew they were big, but I hadn't realised just how much love and affection they inspired.

Not long afterwards, Madness played at the Lyceum. If anything, they were slightly bigger than UB40 and had already notched up quite a few hits in the charts. Everything went well with them – they soundchecked on the day and while I knew the lead singer, the unmistakable Suggs, I hadn't really taken much notice of the rest of the group. There were lots of them as well, just like UB40, but all I did was make sure Suggs had everything he needed and that he was happy with the set-up.

That night, as usual, the queue was right round the building. Another capacity crowd again – about 3,000 people, almost as many as the Royal Albert Hall.

It was a major venue, the Lyceum, and there were always people trying to sneak in to get near their heroes. As it got close to stage time, Cliffy confirmed that the band were in. At the front of the house, I was chatting to Bert when another one of my men came up and interrupted us.

'Roy, would you mind checking this out?' he asked. 'There's a guy here, reckons he's in the band.'

'Oh, don't waste my time!' I told him. 'They've all come in around the side.'

But the geezer waiting outside wasn't having any of it. He was in the band, he said, and he wasn't taking no for an answer. It was up to me to go outside and sort it out. So I looked him up and down: he was just wearing a T-shirt and a pair of white trousers with a green stripe running down them – everyone knew Madness wore suits.

'Can I help you?' I asked, without much interest.

'Well, yeah, you can,' he said, '…if you want the band to play, because I'm the saxophone player.'

'Yeah, 'course you are, mate. See you later. Ta-ta.'

I turned to my man and said, 'Make sure he goes away, will ya?' and shut the door. About 20 minutes later, I was coming down to the stage when my brother blew in my earpiece.

'Where are ya, Roy?'

'I'm near the front, just coming...'

'Nah, nah,' he replied. 'Stay where you are! We're coming to you.'

But he had some news: 'They can't go on stage – it's ten minutes over. They're missing one member of the band.'

'Whaddya mean, missing one member of the band?' I asked, as a light-bulb began to shine in my head.

'Well, there's someone who hasn't turned up. Their saxophone player…'

Suggs arrived. 'We're still waiting for Tommo,' he explained.

I could hear the sounds of an increasingly impatient crowd drifting down the corridor.

'*Mad-ness! Mad-ness! Mad-ness!*'

'What does he look like?' I asked, thinking, *there's no way he's going to describe that bloke sitting outside on the steps with the rest of the fans.*

'He's quite stocky – T-shirt, blondish, cropped hair, white trousers.'

The geezer was still out there. And, I have to admit, he remained as calm as a cucumber. I shambled out to let him in. He was exactly where I'd left him, sitting quietly outside.

Clearly, he'd thought, *Okay, I'll just wait here for you to come to me.*

And he wasn't wrong.

After that, the show went fantastically. Everyone really enjoyed themselves and everything else went to plan. And I made a note to check and double-check in future when someone said they were someone.

I'd been at the Lyceum so long, I was starting to see the same bands come back again. I got on particularly well with the likes of Wham!. I liked George Michael's mum and dad, and I was asked to be George's personal bodyguard.

The band's career was then at its peak and the crowds were phenomenal. George was the really popular one and I don't think many of the fans knew that Andrew Ridgeley's microphone and guitar were switched off – but then again, I don't think they'd have cared, anyway.

One girl chucked a leather hat onstage, just like the one worn by Marlon Brando in *Rebel Without A Cause*. Andrew grabbed it and wore it for the rest of the gig. Afterwards, the fan turned up backstage, desperate to get it back. It belonged to her brother and he wasn't at all happy that she'd thrown it at her idols. She went on and on about it.

I had better things to do than look for a hat, but I glanced around anyway just to shut her up. Andrew gestured vaguely to one side of the room, but I didn't find it. It wasn't top of my list of priorities. The boys needed to get out and I called Cliffy up on the radio and asked him to get the limo round to the back of the building.

I got George Michael in a headlock position, holding him down to protect him with my body against the sea of a thousand screaming, surging, hysterical teenage fans. This was the drill: the stage door would be opened, we would step forward, the limo door would open and I would bend straight forward into the car.

Except – no limo.

No fucking Cliffy either.

As I screamed down the radio at him, I was being torn to pieces. He was only around the front... *The fucking idiot!* By the time he appeared, I could barely reach the car. As I pushed George Michael inside, I felt an almighty crack on the back of my head. My legs buckled, but I managed to get them in. Then they were gone, and that was it.

My head spinning, I staggered back to the Lyceum. There, I put a hand up to my head. It was obvious that I had a really bad fracture – it seemed as if I'd been caught with a baseball bat or a bar, or something. I'll never know if it was meant for me or for George Michael, but I can only think that the owner of the hat had decided to get their revenge.

I had better memories of the award ceremonies we did – there were so many great acts around then. We had to lay on extra security to deal with what seemed like everyone in the business, including Depeche Mode, Spandau Ballet, Duran Duran and one of the first UK female singers to have had a hit in the US. That was Kim Wilde and her big song was 'Kids in America', for which she was nominated for an award. We all thought she would definitely get it, but instead, it went to Duran Duran. Jaws dropped. How could that happen? The reaction was complete shock.

Afterwards, I saw her in the green room. She was really upset; she was crying. I gave her a hug until, noticing that her mum had come in, I gently guided her over so that mother and daughter could commiserate together.

Just at that moment, Cliffy walked in and, seeing I had my arm around the lovely Kim, gave me an eyebrows-raised grin, as if to say, oh, yeah? And I thought, *Oh, for God's sake, behave yourself!*

But he's never let me forget that night. 'Yeah, something went on with you two in there!' he still says. And I always tell him it was just an innocent cuddle, but I don't think he'll ever quite believe that.

The after-show party was loud and great fun. Bonnie Tyler announced that she was going to take to the stage for a 'little sing-song'. That was fine by me. I led her up the stairs, which were quite dark as all the spotlights were on the stage. I could still see that Bonnie had somehow managed to put on odd shoes – one silver, the other gold. I didn't say anything then, but just let her get on with the song. After the applause died away, my curiosity got the better of me.

'Are you making some kind of fashion statement?' I asked, as I led her back to the party.

'What are you talking about?'

'Your shoes,' I said. 'Why have you got different-coloured shoes on?'

As she looked down, you could tell from her face that she had no idea. And she looked like she just wanted the floor to swallow her up, there and then. She admitted she'd got dressed and come out in a hurry, and just hadn't noticed; she thought both her shoes were the silver pair. That was our little thing for that evening – every time we saw one another, we'd laugh.

'*Yeah, dodgy shoes, love*,' I'd hiss at her, as I went past.

Years later, I was in Copenhagen, of all places, when I saw her in the foyer of the hotel that we both happened to be staying in. She was doing one of those eighties revival tours. I strolled over and no sooner had I started to introduce myself than a flash of recognition crossed her face. She still remembered, even after all that time.

'Oh, my God!' she whispered. 'The shoes!'

CHAPTER 7

GOING TO AMERICA

In 1987, boxing promoter the Colonel went to America to look into the prospects for getting into the game over there. He later took Dennis Andries over to defend his title as Light Heavyweight Champion of the World. I'd sparred with Andries when he first signed and went out to watch him defend his title against Thomas 'Hitman' Hearns. Though Andries put on a brave fight and picked himself up off the canvas four times, he was completely out-classed from the first bell. Brave as a lion, he was, but very much a slugger; he would put everything into it and he could throw a punch off the canvas, but Hearns was an awesome fighter – slick, fast and together. His combinations hit like lightning. Pound for pound, he was probably one of the world's best light heavyweights at the time.

If you wanted to make it big in the fight game, America was the only place to be, but you had to get in with certain people who organised it. That's what the first trip was all about. The Colonel's connections in London had given him the introduction he needed and I was to look after him when he went to Little Italy for a meeting. I say that I 'looked after' him, but frankly, I wouldn't have had a chance if it came to anything. I realised this as soon as I saw who it was we were meeting with.

The venue was a restaurant, but if it had a name then I don't remember it. Put it this way, it wasn't the sort of place where you had to book a table! It was straight out of *The Godfather*. There was a guy standing outside with an umbrella to walk people in. A long bar with tables to its right stretched the length of the seating area to a kitchenette at the back and on the far end, was a table at which two men sat. A couple of big lumps were propped up at the bar and they glanced up lazily before giving us the nod.

'Stand there,' I was told, when we reached the bar, while the Colonel carried on, leaving me to wonder exactly what it was that I had got myself into, thousands of miles away from home. I was pretty sure I wouldn't be called on to do anything, which was just as well because I was well and truly out-numbered. I might crack one, maybe another, but then I'd be stuffed. If I'm truthful, I was shitting myself.

The Colonel reached the table and was met by a smartly dressed man with grey hair, who was sitting with a huge guy, wearing a too-tight suit. The smarter man stood up and hugged the Colonel before kissing him on both cheeks – the highest sign of respect. I never liked to ask too much in case I raised suspicion, but I did find out later that one kiss means you're accepted, while two shows you are like family. The Colonel was doing well, which was fine by me, because the atmosphere there was very heavy, and right at that moment I just wanted to get the fuck out of there.

'Can I get you anything?' asked the bartender. It was as if he'd read my thoughts. I could have done with a very large brandy or two.

Instead, I just asked, 'Have you got some water?' The guys around me laughed.

'*Water*?' said one. 'Just get the guy a beer!'

Now I'm a lager man and that's what I thought he meant when he said 'beer', but it was ale. I was about to spit it out in disgust, but the company was so downright terrifying. I didn't want to seem rude...

For a while, the grey-haired man and the Colonel talked quietly before getting up to come down to my end of the bar. The really big guy stayed sitting down. I doubt he could have walked far – he was that huge.

'Oi, Roy, c'mere!' called the Colonel. As I made my way over to him, my legs felt like lead. 'I brought this one over from London. He was a good fighter in his day, knocked a few over,' he said.

His host nodded. 'Maybe you should go and knock about with a few of my guys,' he drawled. 'What do you reckon?'

I looked at the crew surrounding us. 'Every man's got to know his limits,' I said carefully. 'And I've just found mine, standing right here.'

He burst out laughing and said, 'Come here.' Then he took me by the hand and kissed me on one cheek, acknowledging that I'd been quick and sharp in my response. You don't want to think too long before replying in their game otherwise they think you're hiding something.

'You know, you're welcome back any time,' he said. 'We'll have some dinner.'

Yeah, I thought, *I'm never coming back here.* And that was before I found out the name of that grey-haired businessman – the Teflon Don.

CHAPTER 8

WHITE LINES

I drove at top speed across town to deliver the package that someone left behind in Duran Duran's dressing room. Its owner ripped it open as soon as I entered his room and powder spilled out everywhere. Coke.

'What the *fuck's* that?' I said.

'Don't worry,' one of his mates replied. 'It's okay, mate, leave it.'

'Whoa, whoa, whoa! What d'ya mean, leave it? *What the fuck's that*?'

Fuming, I pinned the package's owner against the wall by the scruff of his neck – I had never wanted anything to do with drugs. I stormed out and headed back to the Lyceum, but when I put my hands in my pockets, I felt more of the powder. Having seen how desperate the guy had been to get his hands on it, I wanted to find out what all the fuss was about. I sniffed some of the residue off my fingers.

Fatal mistake.

I had no idea of the years of misery and the damage to my health such an innocent taste would have. *Fuck me,* I thought, *it doesn't half make you come alive! Makes you alert!*

It only seemed like seconds after I finished it off, but it had actually got to 1am. By then, I was hooked.

At first, I started off with half a gram and then it was a gram... all the way up to three grams every day. That wasn't cheap. It wasn't long before it started to affect my work. I became unreliable, bad-tempered and paranoid – not really the qualities you want to see in a big fella like me.

After about a year of shovelling the stuff up my nose, I had a serious problem. I bashed people for no reason at all – you only had to step out in front of me and *bosh!* I'd knock you to the ground. I guess that evil side must have been in my character before, but I'd always managed to control it through the military or boxing.

Now the brakes were off.

'What's up with Roy?' everyone wanted to know. No one knew what lay behind my massive mood swings.

My reputation started to slide and your good name is everything in my game. Bodyguard work tailed off and I had to find money wherever I could. With my new temperament, it was soon only to be found in debt collection and commercial debts, mostly.

I quickly discovered that I was pretty good at it.

Debt-collecting, believe it or not, is an art form. And if you get it right, you can do very well.

I would always go after recent debts before they got too old for their owners to be tracked down. People move on, companies get taken over... Many firms will have just gone bust or rolled so they haven't got to pay VAT, or moved to cheaper premises and set up under a different name. I met all sorts of smart-arses – but though I'd always find them, I quickly realised that it just made life easier to go and collect while the debt was fresh in everyone's mind.

I did quite well by charging about a third of the total amount to be recovered. Well, to be honest, I'd take what I thought was fair and mostly creditors would agree with me. They didn't have a lot of choice. I'd tell them they could have two-thirds in their hand or they could have nothing. The arrogance came as part of the job – I had a couldn't-care-less attitude. That's what I needed to make it work. I couldn't see the point in being nicer to those I worked for than those I took the money off.

I told debtors I was from a company called Debt Direct. It wasn't real, but it sounded good. And I had an extra ingredient – coke psychosis. I became known as an enforcer, a fucking horrible monster. Even if you didn't owe much, I'd go over the top.

One guy didn't have to pay much, but his attitude wound me up. He thought he was the hardest man in south London, a proper gangster. I read him the riot act and he still wasn't having any of it, so I battered him so hard that I'm amazed he survived. He got the message. The next day there was the whole amount on the table – and some more. I took a chunk out of it for myself. My client complained I was taking too much, so now I had the hump with him and all.

'Nah, it's not,' I told him. 'Half is mine anyway and the other half is the cost. You got some money you never had, so just keep your mouth shut because you never know when I might have to come for you if you ever owe.' That was how I was all the time now: constant aggression, bullying, no matter who it was.

My reputation really did begin to precede me. I was taking the lift to one job in an office and I can only guess what I looked like: vacant stare, lost in my own thoughts, sweating from the coke and twitchy.

Someone must have tipped the firm off that I was coming. The lift doors opened and I was faced with a secretary carrying armfuls of files. She took one look at me and the paperwork went everywhere; she was shaking so much with terror that she couldn't even bend down to pick up her work. In fact she looked as if she would have been happy just to drop dead rather than go on feeling that petrified.

And it was all down to me. That was the first time I really began to realise what I had become and what I was doing to myself.

I had become the one you came to for the horrible jobs that nobody else wanted to take on. Guys would come up to me in the pub and have a quiet word, so I made sure I was surrounded by my own lads and I thought I sounded good. I believed my own press and in my madness I even started thinking I was one of the chaps, a proper villain. Now I had become everything I never wanted to be.

Eventually, sometime in late 1987 or early 1988, I was sacked from the job I loved so much at the Lyceum. One night, I came in to find one of the barmaids sobbing her heart out. She wouldn't tell me what was wrong, just said that 'you lot' – meaning men – were all the same.

She was in a right two-and-eight and it turned out it was over the head barman, a suave Italian, who thought he was God's gift. Eventually I got the full story out of her – he'd touched her up earlier in the night and told her they'd be getting together when the shift ended. The poor girl didn't want to stay in the bar a moment longer; she was just about ready to quit her job right then.

'Hold on a minute, he's bang out of order,' I told her, 'he can't be doing that.' Even as I was talking, the man in question swaggered down the stairs.

'You want to go?' he sneered at her, 'you fucking go! Get out of my bar, you're fucking useless!'

He completely blanked me... but not for long.

'Oi, oi, lemon!' I said. 'What's gone on here?'

'Nothing to do with you,' he said, unwisely as it turned out. 'Fuck off and do your own work!'

He can't be talking to me, I thought. But he was, and he went on in the same way until I lost patience and battered him from one side of the club to the other.

Fractured jaw, burst ear drums, broken wrist, broken foot, broken leg, broken nose and broken eye sockets... No denying, he was in a pretty poor state but not so poor that he wasn't wise enough to keep his mouth shut. He didn't know what I would do and he was right to be frightened: I was an animal.

But I couldn't save my job at the Lyceum. They hadn't figured out why I'd changed, they just knew I was beyond reason. Even while old allies like Ron tried to find out what was up, I just snarled and shouted him down. I could see what was coming and I was ready to blame everyone but myself.

'I don't need you, you don't need me,' I said. 'Why don't you stick it up your fucking arse?' I walked out.

What a mug! It looked like my bodyguarding days were over for good.

CHAPTER 9

A CHEAP TICKET

The Colonel had said there was always a job for me in his ticketing agency. That really stuck in my head and when I did go and see him, he was as good as his word. I worked with him, dealing in everything from rock to opera. It wasn't like any office I'd ever seen. His staff included resting actors – some quite famous. I guess the next best thing to working on the stage was selling tickets to go and see performances.

On my first day there, I was amazed to see Derren Nesbitt. He wasn't exactly some jobbing wannabe – he'd been in *Where Eagles Dare* and if you didn't know his name, you'd always recognise him as a character actor. With his bleached-blond hair and prominent lips, he'd typically play the Kraut in one of those movies.

'I recognise you!' I burst out.

'I know, I know,' he sighed, his accent impeccable. 'But you've got to earn a *living*, darling.'

A proper thespian, he was! But he wasn't Derren on the phone, or even Mr Nesbitt. He was Julian – a very thespian sort of name, come to think of it – as none of us used our real identities when we were talking to the customers.

Patrick Holt had been quite big in the 1950s and if you were a fan of the legendary Hammer House production company you'd probably have seen him. Rather than play horror parts himself, though, he was more usually the copper, getting stuck into such terrors as a gang of motorbiking vampires. You couldn't get away from them in the fifties.

The Colonel bought his tickets at source for face value and then, when we sold them on, we added on an agency fee. That's how he made his money and he did very well on it too. But no sooner had I got on the phones that day than the door opened and in came another one of the crew for work: it was only Ray Winstone! I have to admit that one of my all-time favourite films is *Scum*. It was quite bizarre to sit there with him selling tickets to West-End shows like any other salesman in his distinctive voice, but he was a nice guy. Me and Ray struck up a really nice friendship, working together.

I had a regular customer that I'll call Mr B, a multi-millionaire businessman who would often ring up for opera tickets with his unmistakable voice. He was very well spoken, very posh. If he wanted to see a production, he would pay top dollar for a pair of tickets. Not a problem for him. So I knew he was being serious when he told me he was going to be a rival to the Colonel.

'I'm thinking of starting my own agency,' he explained, 'and I'm looking for someone to run it.' He didn't add that he was looking for the most stupid and gullible person he could find to let into his confidence, but he'd certainly found him – me.

'Oh, whereabouts are you thinking of doing this?' I asked.

'I don't know,' he replied. 'I'm thinking about

somewhere in the West End. Would you be able to give me some advice on how to go about it? You probably have good contacts. Someone like yourself would be ideal – I'm impressed by your sales pitch and I'm willing to invest in you.' At least, that's what I *assume* he said – I only heard the word 'invest'. I was only just married then, and I had a kid on the way. Of course, it was no excuse for double-crossing the Colonel, but it was quite some carrot he was dangling in front of me. I knew how much he had.

God, I've hit the jackpot! Somehow I kept my excitement to myself, though.

'Send me money in the post today,' I told him. 'That way I know you're not talking bollocks. Let's get that conversation out of the way.'

But he didn't seem at all concerned.

'Where do you live?' he asked.

I gave him my address and then I went on to sell him whatever tickets he'd called up for as if nothing had happened. Anyway, I didn't think much of it.

Next evening, the missus told me a letter had come.

I opened it up: cheque, a nice few quid. Fuck me!

Immediately, I began daydreaming about having my own ticket office and making the same sort of profit as the Colonel.

Mr B and I met to discuss the new company at the home he shared with his missus and two boys in Chelsea. And what a place it was. Bloody hell! The small rug by the front door looked like it must have cost a small fortune, never mind the furniture, the antiques and the paintings. It all began to make sense to me.

For him, the income from the ticket agency would only be small change. He was probably just bored with what he was doing, needing a bit of excitement.

Well, he was about to get it.

Without letting me know first, he took it upon himself to phone the Colonel the day before the new agency was ready to go: to tell him what he was doing and who he was doing it with.

'It's been lovely doing business with you,' he said to the Colonel, 'and I've spent quite a bit of money over the years.'

'I know,' said the Colonel. 'Are you going away somewhere?'

'Oh, no,' he replied, 'I'm not going anywhere. I've gone into partnership with Roy. We're setting up our own ticket agency.'

You can imagine the Colonel's reaction: *What the fuck's happened here?*

Him and me would be fighting on the same turf for the same thing. Of course, I knew where to go to get the same tickets as he did for the same theatres. I might just as well have gone up to him and stabbed him with a knife – in fact, I might as well have done his whole family. His missus was out shopping when she heard the news and I was later told by mutual friends that she broke down in tears right there and then, in the supermarket, in front of everyone.

Alex Buxton, one of the four legendary Buxton brothers, all boxers, also worked for the Colonel in the ticketing agency. He'd gone up against Randolph Turpin in his day and we had become friends. Or at least he thought we were. 'I *really* can't understand why you're doing it,' Al said to me, 'I thought you were like family.' And I was; I *was* family.

Then the Colonel phoned me.

'How come you're doing this to me, Roy?' he asked, sounding devastated. 'I can't understand...'

'It's not that,' I replied. 'It's just the money.'

'And family means nothing?' he asked. 'Obviously, it means nothing to you, so I suggest you just get on with it. But I tell ya now, you're no longer a member of my family and you never will be.'

And then I realised just how far I'd gone.

It was bad enough that I'd upset the Colonel – and you didn't do that – but it was the way he'd found out. Not from me, not at a moment when I might have been able to explain it, but from someone else, the day before we opened. It was the moment timed to cause maximum upset and offence.

Mr B called me and I had to tell him that the Colonel knew everything. At that point I didn't know *how* he knew it. 'The shit's hit the fan,' I said, and started to explain what had happened.

'Oh, yeah, I know,' he interrupted, casually adding, 'I rang him and told him.'

'*What?*' I asked, very quietly.

'I rang him – I told him.'

'What on earth..? Was it *you*?'

'Well, yeah, I wanted to make sure everything was above board. I didn't want any ill feelings.'

'You prat!' I said. 'I tell you what...'

Bang! I slammed the phone down.

Now I was fuming, absolutely fuming. I went straight round to his house and marched in to tell him what I *really* thought.

'You've got to be some sort of *wanker*!' I yelled. I could see from his face that he'd never been spoken to like that in his life. 'You are the biggest prick I have ever come across and I can't believe you've done that. Did you get some satisfaction out of it?'

'*Well...*' he said, 'I don't think with that attitude that we should go into business together.'

'After all you've done?' I said. 'I can assure you, you will pay me exactly half of what you said was still coming to me because if you don't, I will "pay" you. It's as simple as that. So I suggest that somewhere, somehow, you better find me the dough.'

Without waiting for his response, I left. Sure enough, the very next day exactly the right amount was in my house.

But no amount would repair my connection with the Colonel. *What the fuck was I going to do now?* I couldn't contact anyone in his circle because he would have put the word about: I was an outcast.

All the respect had gone.

I was so ashamed – still am, even today – of the way I disrespected the Colonel, his lovely wife and his boy. They took me in and showed me I could follow another way without using my fists and then I repaid them with treachery.

The Colonel's dead now and I wish, if nothing else, that I could have gone to the man's funeral just to say sorry. I really mean that.

CHAPTER 10

DOOR WARS

The bloke who ran the printers thought he was a bit tasty. He started to argue about the debt he owed. That day, I was coked up and in a bad mood. Come to think of it, I always seemed to be on the gear and angry.

Anyway, I dragged the mouthy bastard over to his own printing press and jammed his head in it.

'If you don't have my fucking money by tomorrow,' I said on my way out, 'I'm going to shove you in the fucking bin!'

You know how you say you're so scared you've shat yourself? The fella literally did that. He knew I wasn't fucking about and the next day, he had the money.

I got a bit of doorman work at a club called Clouds. It was used by Jamaicans and I'm not sure exactly how legit it was, but it was handy for Brixton police station, being exactly opposite – not that they seemed to mind our presence. I didn't bother to try and manage trouble now. At the first sign of aggro, I would smash people all over the place. Not exactly the best way to make friends.

Even at my most violent, the old bill never bothered to

stroll across the road, though the sergeant could have seen us from his desk, had he looked out the window.

One day, I was on my fag break with another bouncer when a car came down the road. As it drew level, the window came down. I was slow now, out of it, and I didn't have any sense of self-preservation... even when a gun was pointed out the window: at me.

The barrel was directly facing me and I stared blankly back.

All that coke made me feel totally invincible and I left it far too late to dive.

If I gave it any thought at all, I suppose I thought the bullet was for the bloke who owned the club. He was just getting in his motor with the night's takings and he'd had an argument with the guy in the car. There was a bit of a turf war going on with a club up the road, who put on a similar night. Who knows? Maybe it was meant for the promoter. But it hit me and perhaps that's who it was for: I was the one who battered them earlier.

As they spirited our guy away, I struggled to my feet then thought to myself, *fuck me, what's that?* I was covered in claret.

There was no way I wanted the old bill involved – they would ask too many questions and anyway, I was carrying coke. So the others at the club got me to a house and gave me some hot water. I needed to get the bullet out – I could feel it in my leg.

The pain was just about bearable, probably because I'd stuffed so much coke up my hooter. It was more the smell that did for me. Rot, burning, dead flesh... Made me want to heave. Concentrating, I used a pair of tweezers to dig around and pulled out the bullet. I knew the wound must be cauterised and if I wasn't going to hospital, I would have to do it myself.

So one of the other bouncers from the club turned on the iron. I grabbed it off him and clamped it down on the entry wound, which was gushing blood. That sealed it and I did the best I could to clean it with some antiseptic cream; that probably hurt the most. The wound was still burning away and I screamed out in pain, then I carefully wrapped it up in bandages.

Next day, it looked pretty messy. The tissue was all soft and the smell was still fucking disgusting, but there was one more job left to do.

The promoter and me took his fancy motor down towards Chelsea, over Lambeth Bridge. As we travelled over the Thames, I chucked the bullet in the river.

By the third and fourth day the flesh around the entry wound had become all hard, so I just put a bit more cream on it. I never did get it properly seen to.

Years later, after a motorcycle accident I had an x-ray in the same area and it showed up fragments of bullet, which penetrated into the shinbone. And they're still there, to this very day.

I've no idea how I would have ended up if I'd gone on like that. Most probably dead, I guess. But the turning point came without fanfares or miracles – it was an ordinary day and an ordinary job.

This woman had run up maybe £800–£900 worth of missed payments on a few domestic appliances. For me, what she owed was nothing more than scratch money as it was getting near to Christmas – I'd be lucky to get anything decent off her full debt and I wasn't thinking much of it. Her son said she'd gone shopping. As I went downstairs, I had a feeling that I was going to be going to a lot of trouble for poxy money. Already, I could feel myself working into one of my now-familiar furies.

I met the woman in the hallway on my way out.

'Are you Mrs Barker?' I asked, explaining who I was and telling her that she needed to make some kind of payment to keep the shop happy. She started to say that she hadn't got anything and as she fed me the usual stories, I looked down at her three carrier bags full of shopping.

'So you're all right to pay for your shopping,' I snapped, 'but you can't pay your debts, can you?' I could see her hands start to shake as I went into my intimidation routine. Nasty, but that's what the business is all about. *It's more likely they'll pay up if they're scared, that's just the way it is.*

'I haven't got much, I can give you what I've got left,' she offered, then attempted to explain herself, talking too fast, scared. 'I've been out of work, but I start back next week and I might be able to pay some of it off every week, if you'd like to come back. Would you mind coming upstairs?'

While she unloaded her shopping, I hung about and she filled the silence with nervous, rapid, small talk. I wasn't interested – I just wanted to get the dough that she owed. But then I started to notice what she was taking out of the bags.

Jesus Christ! She had the smallest chicken you've ever seen in your life. And every tin was own-brand super-value. If you put together the contents of all three bags, I doubt it would come to more than £20. She was just trying to feed her family.

For me, the worst thing about it, the most gut-wrenching thing, was just being there, trying to get a few quid out of someone who'd obviously fallen on really hard times. That day alone I was wearing sovereigns, great big belcher chains and a bunch of what we called chopper-eaters –

massive gold bracelets, some of which I'd taken off people when they didn't have the money to pay off their debts.

'How much is it that I owe?' she eventually asked.

I started to tell her, but even as the figures came out I could hear a change in my own voice. The mindless aggression had gone and I sounded more relaxed, the old Roysie.

'This debt is running up every week,' I told her. 'You'll be chasing yourself unless you can pay a bit more because of the interest.'

'I don't know what I'm going to do, sweetheart,' she sighed. As I was calming down, so was she.

'Look,' I said, 'enjoy your Christmas, because I'm going to tell them not to do anything until afterwards. I'll make sure nobody else comes and we'll leave it until the end of January, and if you can save up a couple of hundred quid, you'll chop the debt quicker.'

I left her to it, but before I'd even got out of the building my eyes had welled up with tears. That poor woman must have been so frightened of this lummox demanding money. There and then, I got into the motor, drove directly to Lambeth Bridge and parked up by the Embankment.

For a moment I just sat in the car, thinking about where I was going. I looked at my reflection in the mirror and I didn't like what I saw: all that gold glinting, it didn't mean anything to me. I knew what I had to do. Taking off all the chains, the rings and the bracelets, I climbed out the car and went over the bridge, then slung the lot in the Thames. I swore I'd never wear anything like that again. Relief flooded through me. Finally, I'd let go and I knew that I'd be strong enough to kick the coke as well.

But I couldn't get Mrs Barker out of my mind.

There was never much chance that the bloke to whom she owed the money would see it the same way as I did.

He couldn't work out why I wasn't going back before Christmas and why I'd let her get away with doing the shopping, but not paying.

'You getting soft or something?' he sneered.

'You think I'm getting soft?' I said, giving him a very particular look. 'Is that what you're saying?' Straight off, he knew he'd overstepped the mark.

'No, no, calm yourself...'

'That woman is probably gonna try her best and she's not going to have the greatest Christmas because of you.' He kept chatting away, but I wasn't having any of it. 'Her debt's cleared. There's no more debt for that woman. Do I make myself clear? If you go near her or I hear that anyone connected to you has gone near her, I'll come for you.'

And he knew I was serious. 'Here, take some of that back. You've given enough,' he said, as I gave him the money I'd collected.

I walked out of the company and out of debt collecting, but I did go back to Mrs Barker's place.

There was an old envelope lying in my car and I stuffed it with the extra I'd just been given and added some more of my own. I posted the money through her letterbox in the entrance hall and called up on the buzzer. Her son answered. 'Check your mailbox, that's all I'm telling you. Check your mailbox now.' Without waiting for an answer, I got back in the car and drove home.

Some time later I found out what had happened to Mrs Barker. There was a taxi firm operating out of Streatham High Road, just next to what was then the Studio and is now Caesar's nightclub. I invested with them, but the association with my business partners, a couple of fellas called Ray and Lol, would later come back to haunt me, although it did quite well for a few months and I was able to trade my own motor up for a Jaguar. Of a night, I would go up and check on how the taxi firm were doing and have a chat with whoever was doing the controller's job.

'Can I have a cab, love?' said the woman behind me. 'I'm just going local.'

I recognised that voice immediately.

'Hello, Mrs Barker,' I smiled, as I turned around.

'Oh, my God! It's you!'

'Yes, Mrs Barker!' I strolled out with her to find her cab, but she wasn't interested in that.

'I'll never forget what you did,' she said. 'And I know it was you! Don't deny it. I had the best Christmas ever.' She took something out of her handbag, which she'd been carrying around since we first met. '*Now* I can give it to you,' she said with satisfaction, handing over an envelope. 'I never knew where to send it.'

I watched as she got in her cab and disappeared into the night before opening what turned out to be a letter.

I don't know why you've done this and I don't understand the method, but I want to say something for all that you've done. I did manage to save some money and now I hear that the debt's been cleared. I can only assume that the debt was cleared by you. My family and I will be grateful to you for the rest of our lives. We can only thank you because I know that you won't accept anything else. And I hope that prosperity comes to you and that your life will change for the better, because deep down, you are a very decent person.

What a lovely thing for her to say! Straightaway, I felt better within myself. I knew I'd done the right thing: Mrs Barker had been chasing her head up her arse for fucking

£20 every month and what was the point of that? The encounter helped me keep to my resolution of staying off the shit.

But I needed to build up some money again.

By the time I quit the gear, I'd put an awful lot of dosh up my nose. When I was a bodyguard I could be clearing a lot, but then I'd spend most of it on cocaine. Factor in the weekends and I wouldn't like to guess what I was getting through a week. I know I'll never be sure how much it was. Cokeheads lie to everyone around them and they lie to themselves too about how much they're going through. It was always easy to tell who else was on coke, because the signals were obvious, but I never admitted that I had a problem to myself. Right up to the moment when I knocked it on the head, I would always tell myself that I wasn't doing that much. I'd laugh it off to mates and tell them it wasn't possible to take that much. But it was. Truth was, I probably spent double what I thought I did.

So much for a so-called 'party' drug!

It's rotted my teeth where I rubbed it on my gums, those teeth that weren't knocked out when I was a fighter – and it's blocked my arteries. When I came off it, I ate like I'd been starved half my life. To be honest, I still didn't find it that hard to clean up, though. It was just easier to knock it all on the head than to carry on the way I was. You have to hit rock bottom before you can start going back up to the top again. It took me maybe a year or fourteen months to sort myself out again, but now I was on my way.

CHAPTER 11

BACK AT THE BON BONNE

My brothers gave me a break I needed. I was back at the club and I was doing doors. It would be a long, hard road, but I was determined to succeed.

At first I was part-time. I needed to get back slowly and I wanted to get back in with my head straight. The Bon Bonne was open all week and it would have been too much for me to go all in.

I took a nice slow weekend – the first one in the New Year, when most people are at home, recovering from the festive season. My brothers gave me an ultimatum: they wanted the old Roy back and they made me promise I wasn't going to do any more of the crap. Too right! I wanted that more than they did.

I swore all the coke and the debt collecting and the *nastiness* was over with, that I wasn't going to push it and end up in a situation where I felt drained again. I would have gone back on the gear to get me through it, but that was bollocks. I had to accept the club wasn't my show any more and I must regain the respect from the bottom up.

My reputation was helpful in some ways. The more

troublesome customers took one look at me and went, '*Fucking hell, Roy's back!*' and they made sure they didn't upset me. And without me, my brothers hadn't been able to handle the tasty families. Whereas I would – I'd go toe-to-toe with them. So they started to behave themselves when they realised they didn't have a touch any more.

To begin with, it was all quite easy for me. On my first weekend back, I even had time to chat with a bloke in the club.

'Can I ask you something?' he said. 'I'm not old bill, I promise ya. Are you Roy Snell?'

'Yeah, that's me. Why?'

'I was just wondering – I work for a company and someone said you might do a bit of debt collecting...'

'I used to,' I said. 'I don't do it no more, mate. You know?' He seemed disappointed and explained that they'd been chasing an invoice and there was always some excuse about it not being right. Now I was curious.

'How much is it?'

When he told me, I was astonished. It was easily enough for me to get back on my feet again.

He said it was a recent debt, only seven or eight months old. There was a good chance I'd be able to recover it and it would go a long way towards helping me get back on my feet.

Things were pretty desperate. All I could afford was a bedsit in Rosendale Road, a few miles away in West Norwood. I had very little money now that I wasn't relying on debt collecting; I didn't even have a car.

Sometimes I had to rely on the generosity of the smashing fella who owned the shop down the road. One night, I'd helped him sort out a problem he had while I was buying the ten fags I could afford. A fella was arguing with the owner. He was three parts gone and threw his change over the counter, hitting the other man straight in the face. A handful of change hurts at point-blank range.

The customer picked up an open can of drink off the counter and, between swigs, started with the drunken, racial abuse.

I just flipped: I grabbed him by the throat and went to push him out the door, but I was so angry that I didn't notice it was shut. He ended up with a cut on his head in a heap on the pavement.

Oh, bollocks! I'd gone over the top – again.

I turned back to survey the damage I'd caused to the shop.

'You best phone an ambulance, he's so drunk,' I called back. Then I reached down and grabbed a can out of the bloke's pocket and poured the booze all over him. With the owner, I cleaned up the shop and we were both standing out front again just as the ambulance turned up.

'Silly bastard tried to run out of the shop with the beers,' I told the medic. 'Gone straight through the fucking window. Silly bastard, look at the state of him!' I was a bit worried that the whole incident might have been filmed, but the shop wasn't fitted with CCTV.

I'd probably caused far more carnage than strictly necessary to sort out the trouble, but the owner absolutely adored me from then on. Still, I never took advantage and made sure I always paid, even though I was down on my luck. Working weekends, I'd only have a couple of hundred quid and yet he always let me settle my bill when I got the cash through. I would always give him a few pounds extra as well, just to show the same respect back.

So there I was in the Bon Bonne, thinking about my tiny bedsit back in West Norwood, about how much better things could be if I just took on one more job. So, I said yes. It was the easiest few grand I've ever earned in my life, not to mention the quickest.

With the paperwork in my back pocket, I walked in the door of the company and was met by the financial director. He explained they were always going to pay the bill, but the creditor wouldn't formally deduct their commission. That was the only thing that had held payment up over all those months.

'Why don't you take the commission off the debt?' I asked.

'Consider it done.'

'Oh.' That was it? 'Really?'

'I'll just get the cheque for you.'

He couldn't have been gone five minutes and I had the cheque in my hands – how quick was that? I was back in the car and off before I'd even had a chance to finish the coffee they gave me.

The guy I was collecting for was a bit of a Jack-the-Lad. He acted like he was one of the chaps, but he wasn't: he was nothing. I could see that the staff in his office believed all his bullshit, though. As soon as I walked back into his place, he was twitching and winking importantly, looking more like Arthur Daley than a genuine villain.

'Follow me, son, follow me,' he said. 'Come in my office. And you lot,' he flicked his thumb theatrically in the direction of his staff, 'Carry on grafting.'

He really was a priceless prat.

'Do you keep a lot of cash here?' I asked, as we sat down.

'No, not really.'

'You owe me my cut,' I said, slapping the cheque down on the table.

He was astonished.

'I'll nip down the bank, Roysie,' he said, wisely.

'Okay, son.'

He came back: jiffy bag, cash. And now, I was back.

I got myself a set of wheels, a sensible set of wheels: immaculate, 1987 Ford Capri, two-door, three-litre Ghia. Leather interior, black over silver. All legit: taxed, insured, MOT – and just 40,000 on the clock, genuine. The car dealer knew me. Now, he was the *proper* Arthur Daley – blonde on each arm, champagne, bag of coke, but smart enough not to mess with the mileage.

'Fuck me, no! I'm telling you, Roy, the last thing we need is you coming down, I can assure you, mate. That's a lovely motor!'

He'd had it priced far too high, but I reminded him of a few favours I'd done him in the past.

So he gave me the big one. 'You're raping me, Roysie, you're *raping* me,' he complained, 'I paid £850.' It was all part of the game.

'Shut up, you tart!' I laughed. 'You paid a monkey for that car.' For half an hour, we bantered back and forth. Finally, I banged the cash on the table.

'And I'll buy the pie and mash!'

He smiled. 'You know what?' he said. 'I've always liked ya, I've always respected ya. You can 'ave the motor, my son.' He just wanted me to go away, thinking he'd done me a favour so he could ask me for something later. That's just how it is: it's all word of mouth all round my manor. No contracts, nothing in writing, it's just understood. He'd given me a good price and he knew that if he had aggro with certain people, then he knew he could always find me at the club and I'd sort it out for him.

So, that was the car ticked off the list, but I continued to be careful with the money. My little brother Cliffy took my box bedsitting room in Rosendale Road and I moved upstairs. There were two rooms, the larger of which I got some fellas to partition into a bedroom and sitting room. The other was a kitchen and they fitted a shower in the corner.

Technically, I'd made my own one-bedroom apartment and it looked the fucking nuts when I'd finished. It really did look nice – nice furniture, colour telly, built-in wardrobe with good-quality wood to hold my suits. Having a decent couple of whistles was a relief.

My new home made me feel better in myself. It was somewhere I knew I could invite someone back for a cup of tea – I was proud to be there. I felt I'd done bloody well to achieve what I had with the space.

CHAPTER 12

CHUCKY

I recognised the fella at the club by sight from the old days on the circuit. He knew me too; he said he'd heard that I'd gone off the rails, but that I used to be quite good at close protection.

'My name's Chucky,' he said.

'That's a funny old name.'

'That's all you need to know,' he replied. He left before his two mates and I asked them who he really was.

'You've really got no idea who that is?' one of them said.

'Well, you know, I've seen him around...'

'He was in Special Forces for years,' he told me. 'He was chief instructor.'

'Really?' I said. '*Fuck me!*' I'd got the feeling he was someone; you could tell by looking at him that he wasn't a regular geezer.

Chucky's story went like this: he came out of the military and set up a company to train bodyguards to the level of Special Forces. His company turned out the highest-ranking bodyguards in the country. The course was tough and the grading recognised by the World Federation of

Bodyguards. But you wouldn't find Chucky's group advertising in magazines or on the Internet. Entry was by nomination: *they found you*. And when they did, they would transform your idea of what it was to be a bodyguard with six weeks of gruelling, intensive training. It was the training used by the SAS and it didn't come cheaply, but the best candidates were sponsored for up to half the fee.

The mysterious Chucky had come along that night to assess my suitability for his elite course and he must have been impressed by what he saw because he came back the next week.

'Have you ever thought of training to be a proper bodyguard?' he asked.

'What do you mean, "proper"? I've been doing it properly all me life,' I said.

'You might think so, but I can assure you, you haven't. You've got a lot to learn, boy.'

Boy! Cheeky blighter. Fucking 'boy'? *Do you know who you're dealing with, son*?

Chucky didn't even look that impressive at first sight. He wasn't the biggest man in the world, not by bodyguard standards. I'd guess about forty-five years old. He was 5'9", a stocky 14 and-a-half stone frame, with a face like a bulldog chewing a wasp.

But I hadn't seen him in action – not at that point. I would find out that he was like a Rottweiler – there was not an ounce of fat on him.

About a month later, Mike – who was a big figure in the industry – and Chucky came down to the club on the same night. Mike came in first and found me inside. We chatted for an hour or so until it was time for me to swap shifts with my brother and take the door. Mike offered to come out with me. Just as Cliffy and Phil went in, leaving us alone, Chucky appeared and walked up the stairs with his two mates.

'Fucking 'ell!' exclaimed Mike. 'How are you, mate?'

'Good to see you,' said Chucky, before turning briefly to me. 'We'll have a word with you later; I've got something for you.'

And they all went in the club together. They acted like it was a coincidental meeting, but Mike and Chucky often seemed to turn up at the club around the same time and if I had to guess who it was who nominated me for the course, I'd say it was Mike, though I'll never know for sure.

I stayed on the door until about half one in the morning – if there was going to be any trouble, it usually started at about that time and that's when I was needed back inside. I went up to my normal place on the plinth at the left-hand side of the club as Chucky appeared with an envelope.

'What's this?'

'Look at it, fill it out. Let me know,' he said. 'Have a pleasant evening, Roy – I'll see you next week.'

He left the club. For the rest of the evening, I felt the weight of the packet through my trouser pocket, but I was on duty so I couldn't do anything.

It wasn't until I got back to my newly converted flat that I was able to tear into the envelope. An application form: what's this? *What a load of bollocks!* But I completed it and handed it back to Chucky the following week. It wasn't long before I got the response – a big, brown envelope full of information, headed: 'Report to Hereford'. The SAS town – Chucky had set up about half a mile from their headquarters and with good reason. As a highly respected former chief instructor, he was allowed to use their equipment as part of his own course.

When we all arrived for the course, we went into a village pub. Sounded like good training to me, but Chucky had read my mind.

'If you think you've come here for a drink, think again,' he said, as we sat down. 'The only reason we're here is to get some grub before we start.'

The landlord came out from the back of the pub. 'Oh, Jesus, more recruits, eh, Chuck?' he joked. 'How many gonna pass this one?' There were eight of us.

'Out of this lot? I reckon two,' replied Chucky, and as he did so, he looked directly at me.

My trademark was my spiked-up hair. Not long into training, Chucky told me he thought it might be a liability, though I couldn't see how. I said as much as well. It wasn't long after that when Chucky happened to be walking past and almost casually pulled me over and down to the ground by my hair. He made it seem effortless.

Point taken. Hair cut. I've had a crop ever since…

From start to finish, the course was tough but I reckon one of the hardest parts was what they called the 'long drag'. This was a timed challenge: you had to get from one point to another and claim a flag without being detected. The course went cross-country with use of roads, major or minor, strictly forbidden. Two teams, red and blue, each had four members and both sides were given 20 minutes' head start before Chucky unleashed a group of fully trained trackers. Anyone detected once had to start again. Get found out twice and you're off the course completely. Go home, that's it. Ta-ta! Failed.

As we started, I swiftly assessed the terrain and decided the only way to get through was to become part of the landscape. I was one of the biggest blokes on the course and I thought I would be the easiest to find, so when I got to the first point, a ridge at the top of a hill, I shifted the bricks in a dry-stone wall and incorporated myself into the scene as best I could. It looked like I was part of the wall. Even if you looked up from the bottom of the incline, you wouldn't see me. Despite this, I didn't think I'd get away with it, but I did.

Then I moved onto the next point, where there was a tree. Again, I just did the same thing: stealthily, I pulled a branch off, covered myself with it and wrapped myself around the trunk. All the trackers saw when they got the binoculars up to that point was... a tree. I'd done it again. Those who just lay along the branches weren't so lucky.

The next location didn't look so promising, but there was a big pile of cow shit. I guessed they wouldn't think of looking for me there – come to think of it, *I* wouldn't want to look for me there either! I didn't even want to be in there, covered in shit, but that's what I did: I covered myself in dung and tried not to be sick.

If it had been a real mission and there had been dogs out after me, they wouldn't have picked up the scent. Well, they would have picked up *a* scent, but it wouldn't have been mine. That's what it was like all the time: I had to think ahead, think on my feet about what was going on around me.

This time, I was one of the blue team and I managed the long drag on four occasions, each within the time limit, and it won me a pass with distinction.

The next task was shooting and that was no problem. I'd been a sharp-shooter in the forces and my ability was second to none. That task earned me my highest mark of the whole course.

By the end of the first week, two of the hopefuls had already been sent home. One more went at the end of the second and by the third, another two had gone. That left just three of us, who all managed to last until the sixth, and final, week. Then, two days into that final week with just four days of the course to go (the seventh being reserved for grading), we had to do the long drag again, but over a much greater distance.

We got to an old building and one of the others decided to tuck himself inside the felt covering the roof. I thought he was pushing his luck when I saw him get up there. He was a much smaller guy than me, though, and I could see what he was trying to do: from a certain angle it was true that he was virtually invisible. Yet who was to say that his pursuers would come from that one direction? There were plenty of ways for them to reach us and he must have known he was taking a gamble. As luck would have it, they did come another way and they immediately saw his outline in the slope of the roof.

Meanwhile, I had found a tree with a massive hole in it and all I had to do was dig down a bit and drag myself up to become part of the tree. It was uncomfortable but somehow I managed to scrunch myself in there. They didn't spot me, not at all! I couldn't see anything, but I could hear the other fella up on the roof getting tagged. I was gutted for him.

Just as Chucky predicted back at the pub, there were two of us left. I won't mention the other guy's name as he went on to get through selection for SAS itself and he's still serving.

On the Sunday I discovered that I'd passed with style – they called it category A-plus with distinction. There were only 18 of us who had ever got that at the time and only 7 in the world with that grade remain.

Finally, I'd done what I'd always wanted to do since I

signed up with the Royal Marines all those years before. I'd always known – physically known it, inside myself – that I could do it. And I had. It gave me even greater respect for the SAS. Not only do those boys do the same course, but they have to go over it every time they get a commission. We did it for six weeks as part of a training strategy for bodyguarding, but they do it over and over again. They're not human; they can't be.

After I'd passed, I got chatting to some of the other guys. Chucky had a pretty impressive bunch. Among his co-trainers was Tommy M, one of the SAS officers who stormed the Iranian Embassy during the siege of 1980.

The guys who pass Chucky's course sometimes have reunions and we heard about someone who didn't pass, but who tried to join in with the lads. They turned him away, but he wouldn't budge. If he was trying to prove his loyalty to the group, all he showed was his disrespect in not accepting his failure to get in. They chucked him out – through the pub window.

CHAPTER 13

MY JOJO

I was at my lowest ebb when Joanne walked into the Bon Bonne. It was January 1992 and I was contemplating yet another year on the doors. It seemed as if nothing would ever change; I knew I only had myself to blame: I had lost my reputation and even the elite training couldn't bring that back overnight, but it seemed to be taking so long to get anywhere.

I'd just be thinking I was getting somewhere and then I would hear a 'but...'.

'I know you're back, but...'

'You say things are different now, but...'

Christ! When the door shuts, it really stays shut. My state of mind was spiralling downwards.

But then, one gloomy January weekend, this girl came into the club and she made my stomach do somersaults. She was only having a quiet night out with her sister, but even then I knew that she was the one for me. There hadn't been anyone in my life since my divorce – well, nobody serious. There were always birds at the Bon Bonne, the sort of women who found the whole doorman thing a bit of turn-on. They liked a powerful man, but each of us knew the score – it was only going to be about a bunk-up or two; I couldn't even tell you their names. But now I realised I was ready for something more. Maybe because I was at my lowest, I was more open and this girl knocked me out.

Me being me, though, I was still a bit of a Flash Harry. I walked up to her and just said, 'I'm going to have a dance with you later, treacle.' And, having just called her 'treacle', I strolled off again. She thought I was an arrogant pig, but I still dragged her onto the dance floor when the slow numbers started.

As we moved together, I learned that 'treacle' had another name – Joanne. She was seven years younger than me. I can't have done too badly because she gave me her phone number at the end of the night. My head was spinning; she was so special.

I could hardly get through the following day; I just wanted to phone her. In fact, I wanted to take her out that same night. *Why wait?*

So, I went to take the number out of my jacket. *Not there!* I had lost her number! At that point, I went completely mad – you wouldn't have wanted to be in my little flat that morning! There was never a more demented man in the history of the world. I tore that place apart, but the number had gone.

Then I started to panic. Maybe she was already thinking that I'd binned her number and that I really was just a bighead, even worse, that I didn't care. I stopped thinking rationally; I even did that thing of trying to guess what the number was. I'd have been lucky to remember one of the digits, but I found myself trying to think of likely groups of numbers. Who was I fooling? I hadn't even looked at the number the previous evening.

So it was back to the waiting game – but this time I was waiting for Joanne rather than a job. That night, I rushed to work, but she didn't come to the club, which left me hanging on until the following weekend. It was agonising, and still she didn't come back. Not a sign of her. *Oh... bollocks!*

The following Friday I scanned the queue outside the club. There was always a huge line for the Bon Bonne and that night was no different. By then I had given up all hope. *But she was there, about halfway down the snaking line of people with her sister!* I was the happiest man ever. So I explained what had happened and she gave me an extremely unsympathetic hearing.

'Yeah,' she said sarcastically. 'Bollocks you lost my number! You just threw it away.'

I had been right – I knew she'd been thinking that and this time I made sure I kept a tight hold of her number. It wasn't going to happen again.

We started dating. I moved out of Rosendale Road and into quite a big house in White Horse Lane, down in South Norwood, which belonged to a friend of mine called Jerry. I paid a token rent and agreed to do the place up for him.

Unfortunately for Jerry, my DIY abilities are shit, but at least I had somewhere affordable. And I was pretty good with paint. I did a deal with a bloke on a building site. The only colour he had was blue.

'*Christ!*' said Cliffy when he saw the results of my work. 'Have you got a tank of everlasting blue in the garden?' The entire house was blue: every wall, every ceiling.

My cooking skills are on a par with my decorating and I'd tried to keep it simple when Joanne first came over, very simple: Steak House grills, mash and beans. Halfway through the preparation I realised: *Shit! I only have one plate, one knife and one fork!* But it was too late. I dished hers up properly and ate mine out of the frying pan. I'd hoped she would feel something for me – pity, maybe, if not love.

The next week she chucked me, but it had nothing to do with my culinary talents – or lack of them. She had simply seen me at work in the club and she was uneasy about the kind of person I might turn out to be. She'd seen my darker side when I got into a row and went toe-to-toe with a punter outside. It wasn't a pleasant sight. She didn't like that side of me and she didn't want to get to know that Roy.

I was gutted, absolutely gutted. I could have kicked myself. *Here we go again.* I was struggling to get up the career ladder and now I was sure that I would never be able to hold down a relationship with the one woman I knew I loved.

I started to take it out on punters at the club. It was completely out of order, but I was out of control. At closing time, one fella asked me if he could finish his drink and I was immediately full of fury.

'You're going *now*,' I told him. 'Never mind finishing your fucking drink.'

'Oh, for fuck's sake!' he said in exasperation. He put the drink down – and I chinned him. Now, why did I do that? I couldn't even say he was arguing the point. He was on his way out and I decked him anyway because I was upset about Joanne.

But I couldn't keep using other people as an excuse. I had to come to terms with myself. This was me, this was my nature; I had to learn to control it. I'd never be a bodyguard if I couldn't.

My brothers started to take notice when I hit that geezer.

'For fuck's sake!' they told me. 'Not again!' They all thought I'd gone back to my old ways.

Phil came up to me at the end of the night. 'Look, I've gotta ask ya,' he said. 'You're not back on the shit again, are ya?' I'd been so violent and unreasonable. That really hurt, though, that Phil would think I was back on the coke. And if I wanted to prove to Joanne that I wasn't the violent bastard she thought I was, I was going the wrong way about it.

The following Friday I was in the club in my civvies – no Dickie or tie or suit – when it kicked off with a bunch of scaffolding boys. And boy did it kick off. They do like a row, those lads, but in this case one of them had taken a liberty with a girl in the club. She'd gone to the fag machine and as she was distracted, one of the lads lifted her skirt up. He made some comment about her underwear and she felt totally humiliated and disgusted. She made a complaint to my brother Cliffy.

'Listen, lads,' he told them, 'I'm not having that. You've gotta go.' It was just him at the table with six of them. And scaffolders aren't little. One of them stood up and bang, they were off! Phil came flying in, Lee dived over the bar and I – on my night off – heard all this from the bar.

'Right, let's go,' I said to my mate.

I put my drink down and charged over to the dance floor.

One of the regulars saw me closing in.

'You're in trouble now,' they told the scaffolders. 'Roy's coming.'

They weren't wrong.

Bang! One down! *Bang!* Two down! *Bang!*

Three punches, three of those lads out cold.

One of my brothers was outside with another of them, the two of them going back and forth.

'Will you fucking stop piss-balling about?' I said. The geezer kept coming back at him. I pushed my brother out of the way, looked at his opponent and said, 'Try me.'

Bang! Number four.

The remaining lads were terrified. 'Easy!' they shouted, 'Easy! Leave it!'

'Leave it?' I said. 'You think you're hard? I'll take each and every one of you outside, individually or all together. Let's have it, us lot.'

Even my brothers were saying, 'Leave it, Roy!'

'Nah, nah, nah,' I told them. 'I'm not having none of these cunts thinking they can take the piss in here.' I turned back to the lads. 'Four of your pals are sparko. You're *that!* None of you have any balls between ya. I'm gonna take your heads off, one by one.'

And one of the boys said, 'Listen, Roy. We're not gonna fight ya. There's no way we're gonna fight ya. You can bash me right here and now, but there's no way I'm going to fight ya. My hands are down; do what you gotta do 'cos all I wanna do is get my pals out. All I wanna do is get 'em home.'

My brothers agreed. 'Please, just leave it', 'You're not even working', 'Just go back inside…'

My back was up, but I went back inside. 'Do yourselves a favour,' I told the scaffolders as I walked off. 'Get that shit outta the club! And don't come back for a fortnight because you're barred.'

As far as I was concerned, that was the end of it. But I didn't know that I'd hit one of them so hard that the bone had come through his nose and another had his jaw completely dislocated. He couldn't even speak.

Before the evening was out, the place was stormed by a mob of old bill. I thought I might not be picked up because

I wasn't in my work gear, but two of the customers piped up, 'Over there, the one you want to talk to is that fucking psychopath. He's the one who did most of them. Fucking nuts, he is!' I couldn't believe it. Both girls were regulars and they'd only been chatting away to me earlier.

The sergeant said, 'And you are?'

I smiled: 'Roy Snell.'

'What, *the* Roy Snell?'

How had they heard of me?

I guessed I was under surveillance and that the sergeant had just let the cat out of the bag. It seemed to me that my door work, bodyguarding and debt collecting hadn't gone unnoticed. The police who covered the West End and the Lyceum would have known the local Peckham coppers and they'd all drink together. Word gets around. They'd seen me with the Colonel and some of his associates as well.

But I also knew they didn't have anything on me.

It was up to me to explain what had happened and how I'd got involved, even on my night off. I wasn't going to deny it – I couldn't. I showed them my hands and anyone could see my knuckles were up.

'You've done quite a bit of damage, haven't you?' the sergeant remarked.

'Well, I'm not here to fucking pussy-fart-arse around, am I?' I said. 'I'm sure they would have liked to have done the same to me, but they couldn't.'

There was a detective inspector with him. He turned to his sergeant, saying, 'Nick him! He's under arrest for ABH and GBH.' *Oh, for fuck's sake! No, not again!* They took in everyone who'd been working security that night. Meanwhile, I cooled off in the cells before being called out for interview to go over the events for what seemed like the millionth time.

'I whacked them... They whacked us... I got the better of them... Tough shit,' I said. 'They wanna press charges? Let them press charges – I couldn't give a fuck! All I wanna do is go home. I'm tired, it's half three in the morning. And if you're not gonna let me out, put me back in the cell and shut the fuck up because I wanna get some sleep.'

The detective inspector, whose name was Sharp, came in and he started on a new subject.

'Right,' he said, as he sat down. 'Do you know a certain gentleman by the name of Raymond?'

'*Raymond?*' I was puzzled. 'No.'

'What about Laurence?' Not a glimmer.

He laid out photos of each of the two men and a third shot of them with me. Now I remembered! *Ray and Lol!* They were the two guys that I went into the mini-cabbing business with in Streatham. Now I knew why the police had been following me.

'Would you like to let us know what these two gentlemen are up to?' asked DI Sharp.

'I'm not their fucking mother's keeper, am I?'

I'd known Ray and Lol were up to something when we worked together, but I'd been careful not to poke my nose in. It was none of my business. The DI tried to pursue it, but even he could see that I hadn't got a clue.

Ray and Lol turned out to be proper villains. Their side of the minicab business was just a front. Later, I heard that Laurence was stabbed 16 times coming out of a Margate nightclub and died. The last thing I heard about Ray was that he was an ill man; I don't know if he's still alive.

Almost a month later, I was told to report back to the police station to hear whether charges would be brought. DI Sharp was waiting for me at ten o'clock that Saturday morning. The desk sergeant told me that none of the scaffolders had chosen to take their complaint further and therefore, I was free to go.

'You got a minute?' asked DI Sharp. I wondered what was coming now. 'My daughter's having her 18th birthday party.'

'Right...'

'And I'd like you to work the door for her.'

After all he'd done to me! Arresting me, accusing me of being involved with a gang, questioning me relentlessly about my associations... And now he was asking me to work on his daughter's bloody birthday! So I did.

It was a church hall do and by any standards, it was trouble-free. I think Sharp was just like any worried dad: he was concerned about his daughter and her friends with all the lads around. There was that zoop-zoop rave music scene then. Rather than use his colleagues, who might get disciplined for moonlighting, he had called in Roy Snell. I was the deterrent. Best kind...

The birthday girl turned up in a car with her mother.

'Ah, you must be Roy Snell?' said Mrs Sharp.

'Yes, that's me.'

'My husband will be along in a little bit. He's just coming off duty.'

'Yeah, well, everything's tickety-boo now,' I said.

The daughter said earnestly, 'I've heard a lot about you. Honestly, there won't be any trouble – I've told my friends what my daddy said.'

'What's that, then?' I asked.

'Not to mess with you!' she said. 'We've got to be on our best behaviour or we'll be in serious trouble and Daddy says there'll be nothing he can do to help.'

The result was the best-behaved rave in the history of pop culture. The kids even finished 15 minutes before they were supposed to and trotted out, chatting away happily. They'd had a great time.

'Keep your voices down,' I warned, ''cos there's people trying to sleep around here.' *Bang!* They all shut up instantly. It was hilarious, like someone had pressed the mute button on the telly. Not a peep.

DI Sharp had agreed a fee with me, but at the end of the night he handed over a bit more.

'That's very good of you.'

'You're worth every penny,' he said, 'and I take back whatever's been said. I don't care what they say about you: you're a nice fella, there are nice things about you. Keep doing what you're doing. And stay straight – there's no need for you to go any other way.'

'I know that, but I get circumstances beyond my control.'

'What? Breaking someone's jaw and fracturing someone else's nose?' he barked. 'Little bit over the top, Roysie, even *you've* got to admit that!'

'Well, you know,' I said, 'I don't hold 'em when I throw 'em.'

'There's no need for it,' he repeated. Tapping his head, he added, 'Use this – not those.' He gestured towards my fists and walked off. I never forgot what he said.

It was back to the Bon Bonne on the Sunday night for my regular job and I was at home on Monday afternoon when someone knocked on the door. That was unusual in itself; I didn't get visitors.

Joanne.

She held out a jumper. My jumper, a black polo-neck.

'This was in with my stuff,' she explained.

'You've come all the way over here just to bring that?'

'No, not really,' she admitted. 'Thought I'd come in and talk with you.'

The Bon Bonne world was small and someone must have told her how bad I was feeling about everything and how much she meant to me. I've never found out how she knew what was going on with me. To this day, she refuses to tell me.

She came in the house and gave me the jumper and I didn't let her go. We've been together ever since that day.

We decided to get married in the summer, two years later. I was still working in the club and I wasn't earning the sort of money that I needed to get the wedding we wanted. The only way I could raise the cash was go back into debt collecting.

Phil worked for a major printer in south London with a book of outstanding invoices totalling a vast amount.

'But you can't go around sticking people's heads in the press,' he warned. 'You can't do that, bruv! You've gotta do it properly.'

He took me to the huge industrial site where the printers sat and introduced me to the guv'nor. The fella was a dead ringer for Dudley Moore – he was his double! So I told him straight out and it did break the ice.

'Dudley' backed up what Phil had said: there was to be no aggro. Their clients included the likes of Sainsbury and Tesco. They couldn't afford to have an enforcer going around bouncing people off the four walls.

He opened a safe and took out a bulging folder with all the information on the money they were owed. Some of the debts went back four or five years. Straightaway, I told him that I wasn't interested.

'Anything more recent?'

'I've got some which are a few weeks old,' he said, leafing through the notes, 'and some of them go back a year... two... three years.'

Aha! I thought. *That was more like it. Nice little stretch of debts there.*

'How much are the newest ones?'

He picked up the papers at the top of the pile and started reading. All I could hear was wedding bells – paid for. He interrupted my daydream.

'I've got another firm willing to do it,' he said. There was a proper debt-collecting agency with bailiffs and all that malarkey. Their commission was 10 per cent, but I could have the job if I accepted the same deal.

That was a hell of a drop in pay, but he did have lots of debts to take 10 per cent out of and each of them was for a big sum. I had a wedding to pay for, so I told him I'd do it.

Then I had to tell Joanne.

'I'm going to be straight with you, darling,' I told her that night. 'I'm not gonna lie to you. We need to find the money for the wedding.'

She told me not to worry and explained that her dad was going to chip in.

'It's not that, I'm a proud man.'

I wanted her to have a day fit for a princess. Why? Because she was.

She was very reluctant to give me the go-ahead and made me promise that it would only be until the wedding was paid for.

'No more,' she said firmly. 'You're never doing it again. It stops.'

And she was right: the printer would be the last person I'd do debts for.

Joanne insisted on coming with me. I thought she was nuts.

'Otherwise I don't want you to do it,' she said. She was

serious – she knew I might turn when someone promised to pay one week, but then didn't; I might get the hump. She would be able to calm me down.

Joanne was as good as her word. She came with me every week.

Some debts were paid in full and others worked off gradually. One bloke paid almost everything straight up. The rest he'd do over a few weeks. That was handy.

I went back with the money and waited for my share.

'The debt's not cleared, Roy,' said 'Dudley Moore'.

I was used to taking my percentage from each payment.

'That wasn't the agreement,' I told him.

'I thought I made it clear,' he said. 'I'll definitely give you the money, but there's still more to pay. Soon as he's paid...'

'I'm trying to pay for a wedding here,' I interrupted, 'and I need the money sooner rather than later. I can't agree with that. Tell you what, I'll take it back and you can stick it up your fucking arse, you twat!'

He went to the safe and gave me my money. I got enough to pay for the entire wedding just from that piece of work.

I stayed at Cliffy's the night before the wedding and woke up to rain while Joanne was back at the house having a champagne breakfast with her friends and sisters.

It was still cloudy when we got to the big, beautiful church in Sydenham – my dad, Judy, Lee, Phil, Cliff and my mum. But not my sisters or my eldest brother Steve – I'd fallen out with them by then. The whole of Joanne's family turned out, though – and she's got a big clan.

As the music started, I turned around to see her. Her hair... her dress, embroidered with pearls. It was perfect. As she approached, the sun reached down into the church and touched her – it was amazing. My legs started to go.

Dad was behind me.

'Don't you *dare*!' he said. 'I'll kick your fucking arse...'

'Not in the church, Dad!'

'Get yourself back there, boy,' he growled. 'Put your shoulders back. Make me *proud!*'

He turned round to see Joanne and burst into tears.

'*Jesus Christ!*' he blubbed. '*She's beautiful!*'

That started Mum off and I felt myself welling up too. I just couldn't believe what a lucky fella I was. As she reached me, Joanne started to fill up too. Everyone was in pieces. The vicar looked like he couldn't quite work out what was going on. Tears of pure happiness, everyone felt the same – they all sensed it radiating out from us.

I'd got a vintage 1912 Rolls Royce for the journey to the reception in a massive hall – biggest place ever.

All the well-known faces from the manor came – it was a proper who's who. And everyone from the printer's – they were all my brother's workmates and if it hadn't have been for them, I wouldn't have been able to pay for it. Even 'Dudley Moore' got an invite.

Down you come, son. Have a few sherbets!

The next morning, JoJo reminded me of my promise: 'Your debt collecting is over. I never want you to debt-collect again.'

'Okay, sweetheart.'

CHAPTER 14

PERSONAL PROTECTION PROMOTIONS

When the Bon Bonne was sold under our noses, I knew I needed another source of income. And fast. The answer came in the shape of Mr J, who ran a chauffeur company and needed a driver. That suited me just fine. Mr J wore a full-length leather coat and had a blacked-out BMW 7 Series motor. I think he half-fancied himself as a bit of a gangster but there was never any aggro driving him. Most days, I just sat there reading the paper.

Then we picked up his business associate, who was into two-way radios and security equipment. As soon as they started chatting away in the back of the car, I recognised his voice. I looked in the mirror. *Fuck me – it was only someone I'd had to turn upside down during a debt-collecting job!* I hadn't seen this guy for donkey's years. And the last time we met, his head was upside down in a bucket.

'You ain't met my new driver,' said Mr J. 'This is Roy: Roy Snell.'

I watched the geezer's reaction in the mirror. His eyes opened wide and locked with mine. Pure terror filled his face. He tried to say, 'Yes, I know Roy,' but he seemed to have developed a stammer and couldn't get the words out.

'How... How... How are you, Roy?'

But Mr J had no idea what was going on. 'What's the matter with you?' he said.

'Listen,' I said. 'It's been a long time. Forget it, mate.'

'I'm fine, I'm fine,' he gabbled, 'I understand, I'm okay...'

'It was a few years ago,' I said to Mr J. 'Your friend needed a bit of friendly persuasion to part with a few quid he owed someone else...'

Mr J interrupted with a great belly laugh.

'How embarrassing is this?' he said.

'Well, not for me,' I replied. 'And it shouldn't be for him either. What's done is done. Now, let's just forget it. We don't need to go into details.'

But Mr J was intrigued by my past. It got him thinking.

'Debt collector?' he said to me later. 'I didn't know anything about that.'

'Before you say it,' I said, 'I know what yer gonna ask. And the answer is, "No."'

'And what's this about you being a bodyguard?' he continued.

'Yes, I was. I was also damn good at it until I spoiled meself. I was an idiot.'

'Why's that?'

'Let's just say I got wrapped up in summat that I shouldn't have done. At the end of the day, it nearly destroyed me.'

He guessed I meant the cocaine.

'Oh, fuck me... we all do *that*! Fucking 'ell, as it happens, you don't fancy one, do ya?' He pulled out a stash of cocaine and I had to tell myself to be strong. *No, Roy, no!*

But he never left it alone. He'd always try to tempt me.

'I've got a little bit,' he told me, almost every day. 'If you ever fancy a bit, you've only gotta let me know and I'll give you some.'

He liked the glamour and he liked the idea of having someone as highly trained in security as me. It wasn't long before we were discussing the idea of him adding a bodyguard division to the cars. And it wasn't just talk with him. He might have been young, but he was very wealthy. It was only later that I found out his dad owned a major cinema group.

'How much would it cost to get the bodyguards going?' he asked.

The easiest way to tell if he was really serious about the idea was to work out exactly how much it cost – and then double it. So that's what I did. But it didn't seem to put him off.

'If I was to say I was interested in fronting it up as a partner, what would you say? What would the split be?'

'If you're gonna front all the money, it's only fair that it would be fifty-fifty,' I told him. 'I haven't got that type of money, that's for sure.'

'Let me think about it.'

That Friday, he told me he didn't need me to drive him anymore. A new bloke was taking over. He asked me to spend a few days in the car control room of the company offices, get the feel of the place.

But I didn't connect it with our conversation earlier in the week. I had no idea what he was talking about.

'Take a good look at the chauffeur circuit,' he added. 'See what you think.'

All right then, so he was paying. After the weekend, I introduced myself upstairs and chatted with the controllers about the various drivers. But there wasn't really much for me to do, and come Thursday, I was still wondering what the fuck was going on.

Usually, I wandered in around half nine. I didn't have to clock-watch, I just walked in whenever I felt like it. About 20 minutes later, one of the controllers called out, 'Hey, Roy, the big boss is on line one for you.'

It was Mr J.

'Hello, Roysie. Where are you?' he said.

'I'm upstairs in the control room.'

'What do you think of the chauffeurs?'

'Well... I'll be honest, I can see room for improvement with some of them.'

'I'm down in the main boardroom,' he said. 'Would you mind coming down?'

Mr J and some of his colleagues were waiting. Tim, the finance director, had drawn up some contracts, which Mr J wanted me to look at. *Contracts?* My head was spinning. Everything seemed to be moving so quickly. I had no idea what they were talking about. Was this my dream? Was I about to become the bodyguard I'd always wanted to be? Was Mr J serious?

'Oh, by the way,' he said, 'I thought I'd go for that rather than what you said.'

He handed me a contract. It was everything I'd asked for – and more. I walked in with 10 quid in my back pocket and now I was walking out with my own division of the company to run as an elite bodyguard organisation, cars included.

I went home and told Joanne.

'Oh, my God!' she said.

'Yeah, exactly – "Oh, my God!" I haven't got a clue.'

But now I had to do it, now I had to make it happen. I

just felt scared. Why was I feeling so scared? This was the opportunity I'd been waiting for, but it was a hell of a responsibility and I knew I had to prove myself.

I even thought of a name: Personal Protection Promotions was born. PPP.

Our office would be the chauffeur control room. So *that* was why I'd been told to spend a few days up there looking at how it all worked.

We offered the whole package: car and security. Whenever I needed equipment, I would phone up the guy who'd been so frightened of me in the car. Mr J did a lot of business with him and he was always very eager to get me anything I needed – not least because he was still petrified. Bless him!

The first bloke I recruited as a bodyguard was Ronald Killick – and I still absolutely adore him. That man went through more than most with me. Ronnie was a damn good bodyguard, but talk about a Labrador! If you kicked him, he'd come back for more – and I did. Whenever he made the slightest mistake, I'd rip his arse off – he was my number two, so he wasn't allowed to make the same error twice. If anyone embarrassed me then by Christ I'd come down on them like a ton of bricks – even him! But he would stick by me, as it turned out, more or less to the very end.

We ploughed through piles of CVs to assemble a team of the best. Most of our guys would be ex-Special Forces. That would be the key difference with my firm: Ronnie and me made sure we never just employed that lump from the gym with the attitude and the steroids.

Those fellas might look the part, but what good were they? Okay, if they got hold of you, they had the bulky muscle to cause you trouble, but if you get to them first –

snap! You could break their legs. Why? Steroids cause brittle bones. And even at the best of times, those guys could hardly run ten yards before running out of puff. *No use at all.*

I tell you what, though. There were a lot of lumps about in the industry. You didn't need a licence to be a bodyguard and that meant the industry was full of pumped-up wannabes who would lie about what they'd done. They'd get their mates to cause trouble and then they'd wade in and look like they were doing a top job. Result? Moody firm gets contract renewed and rich client thinks they're being protected. But they're not. I kept seeing those same chancers getting away with it and strutting about like they owned the place, but the truth was, they were a danger to everyone.

They didn't know how to read a situation; they weren't good enough to anticipate trouble, to be ready for something unexpected. To be a proper bodyguard, you have to see what's about to happen long before it does.

Ask yourself this: you've taken a client for an evening out. Who's going to pose a risk to them? You might be surprised at the answer. It's not the dedicated fans. It's the posh bloke in the bar who's downing bottles of champagne next to your glamorous client. Give him a bit of boozy courage and he'll be the biggest pest of all.

So you don't want to wait until he makes his move. Otherwise you'll be forced into a situation where you might have to give him a clump when you didn't need to cause any aggro. All you have to do is calmly ask your client if she wants to stay or move on somewhere quieter. And if she wants to stay, it's down to you to make your way over to the bar and tell the staff not to serve the troublemaker.

My client is the star. When she comes in, she owns the building.

And that attitude was to pervade my company. My guys wouldn't just look the part – they could save your life in any situation.

No expense was spared to promote PPP. We got a lavish brochure to advertise our services and I targeted our market with precision. We would only do close protection. No door work, gigs or general security, it was only going to be the VIPs.

We charged prices accordingly, well above what you'd expect to get for regular work.

'Roy, you'll never get that, mate,' said my friends. But I had the best men and I knew that my clients would be prepared to pay for the best.

So I sat back and waited.

I'll never forget that first call: Elstree. The head of production on *EastEnders!* She needed us to provide cars and security for PAs – personal appearances. The stars were paid to turn up at nightclubs or cut a ribbon to open a building. And we got the contract to cover the whole cast.

I put the phone down.

Yes, we're up; we're running! Fuck me!

And working for one of the biggest soaps in the country.

CHAPTER 15

THE BRIT AWARDS

'Hello, Ms Driver, my name's Roy Snell,' I said to actress Minnie Driver, as she got out of her limo. 'I'm head of security here. I'd like to escort you to the party.'

I nodded towards the paparazzi, waiting for a glimpse of the rich and famous.

'Are you okay with the press?'

'Yes, fine, thanks for asking, though,' she said.

'You're welcome.'

She was a lovely lady, very down-to-earth. As I walked her to the fashion show VIP area, I told her about the services we provided and asked if she'd mind me giving her my card.

'No, not at all, please do,' she said. 'Thanks very much, I appreciate it.'

Maybe she would give out my name when she got back to the States? Who knows, but one thing was for sure: PPP was starting to get some great VIP gigs.

Whenever my company did security for a big show I would always stand somewhere prominent and hand out business cards to the stars. I got to know a guy called Sasha Levy, who did chauffeur cars. Each of them had a numberplate with his company letters on it. He had some big names. Ronnie Wood, Rod Stewart, Shirley Bassey; they all used him regularly and they all came without security. I was hoping this would be my opening.

Sasha and I got chatting at a charity do in aid of lymphoma at the Langham Hotel, near Oxford Circus. Our lot unloaded the *EastEnders* actors and then Sasha turned up with the likes of Mick Jagger, Stella McCartney and her fashion friends. I gave each of them a card and they all seemed very interested. I was feeling very confident – I must have dished out 80 or 90 of my ads to the biggest stars in the UK in just one night.

It was the designer who was first to use us. As soon as I gave him the details, he told me that he was staging a fashion show in a couple of weeks.

'I might be interested in using your guys. I didn't really know where to go.'

What a touch! He was practically the first guy I met and he came across. We would handle the VIP section for his do and it was a big one – Stella McCartney was going to be there, Vivienne Westwood too and that was where I met Minnie Driver.

On the night of the show I did what was called the walk-down: that was when I'd accompany each star from the car to the VIP area. It was also my chance to talk to them, get a bit of banter going and push the company's services.

My earpiece was buzzing by the time I'd sat Minnie Driver down.

'Roysie, Roysie, Jerry Hall's here!'

I did the same thing, starting with a very friendly sales pitch as we made our way to the party. She wasn't too pleasant, I have to admit. You know when someone's genuine and although she was polite enough, I could tell she wasn't listening to a word I said. Oh, she nodded and agreed in all the right places, but she didn't want to talk to me.

Cat Deeley was next up. She arrived with a blonde friend. I started to go into the routine.

'My name is Roy Snell and I'm head of security, and I want you to know I'll be taking care of you tonight.'

She looked me up and down.

'*All* night, babes?' she asked, with a suggestive grin.

I laughed: 'Don't start any of *that*!'

It broke the ice. She was such a sweetheart, a really lovely girl.

'Give me a few of your cards,' she said, ''cos I'm going to America soon and if I hear that someone's coming over here, I'll give them your details.'

And she meant it. She became a dear friend of mine and she still lives out in LA. She's promised to fly over especially when I launch this book.

Talking with her was an example of the way I developed my own style of working. It wasn't necessarily by the rules, but it was unique to me and that got me noticed. Ronnie, my number two, he saw it too, but he knew that he couldn't try the same thing.

Some of the new guys took a bit longer to see how it worked.

I would build a rapport with people and that gave me a certain licence, but I'd done that from the day I started the company – having had a bit of a laugh with someone like Cat. I could take the Mickey out of her and she'd give as good back.

'Come 'ere, darlin',' I'd tell her sometimes, 'you've got a lovely pair of la-las!'

But she wouldn't take it to heart. It was just Roy.

When the other lads tried it, Ronnie soon put them in their place. You had to earn the position I had, but the stars liked my cheekiness. They kept coming back to us and I think that's why the business became as successful as it did. I didn't wrap them in cotton wool and I wasn't a yes-and-kiss-arse-man – I would say what I thought.

And yet I wouldn't say no just to be awkward. I always did things sensibly and they respected that.

'Listen,' I'd tell them when they got out of line. 'We're not doing that! Don't be fucking stupid because you're putting me, yourself and the rest of us in danger. Now think about what you're doing and think about what you're saying, you fucking idiot! And if you don't want to listen, get someone else to do your security. Stick it up your arse 'cos I'm not interested.'

I could see my other boys thinking, *he can't talk to them like that!* But then they'd see the client agree with me.

That was me; that was the way I was – I would tell it straight from the start.

I had found my feet and the money started to come in. Finally, we were able to decorate my place properly – no more everlasting blue! When Joanne finished with the house, it looked the nuts: there were new carpets, new everything. Each day, I felt better about things and the jobs seemed to keep getting more and more prestigious.

My company was given the VIP section at the Brit Awards ceremony. It was over in Docklands on a boat moored at one of the quays and I got the gig for doing the walk-down.

I made sure I checked out the location beforehand. The ceremony was to be held below decks in a massive ballroom. I went over the list of guests. My first client was an American singer. She was quite a stunning lady – though I'm not going to give her name away here – and when I met her that night, I discovered that she was also a down-to-earth person. I gave her my card when she said that she was over for a few days and was after some security.

She turned in a fantastic performance and the audience absolutely loved her. As soon as she came off stage, I met her and walked her back to the dressing room.

Coming down the corridor from the opposite direction was Whitney Houston and her head of security and former personal bodyguard, Bernie. I'd met him on the circuit and we'd become friends. Originally employed by Whitney's aunt, Dionne Warwick, Bernie was very well-respected in the entertainment world – he appeared in her movie *The Bodyguard* as the man who employs Kevin Costner.

It was hard to stay professional when I saw an old mate like Bernie, but you can't start chatting when you're on duty and so we marched past one another without a glance.

As soon as we'd both dropped our charges off in their respective rooms, we dashed back out to the corridor.

'*Roy!*' he yelled. And he had a big voice.

'How are you, mate?' I grinned. 'Nice to see you! How are things?'

He was just getting into doing *The Bodyguard*.

'The movie is all about you guys,' he drawled. 'It would be great to get some tips, you know, because we need to train Kevin Costner.'

That made me laugh. The whole idea of a film called *The Bodyguard* seemed strange to me. It was just a media term – professionally, we're known as Close Protection Officers, or CPOs. But Bernie wanted me to advise him on how things were done to help create a sense of authenticity.

Bodyguarding was basically the same all over the world, but there were some important differences in the way that the US and UK did the job. For that reason, American stars had to employ British bodyguards because the police had got sick and tired of the aggression of their US counterparts. Not only were they more forceful, but they also took advantage of different traffic laws, which allowed them to take out cars in formation and run red lights. You couldn't do that over here.

Well, most of the time, anyway.

When I got caught in a traffic jam behind a crash I was driving a certain gentleman in the back of the car – a Mr RS. I crept onto the hard shoulder and snuck through to the front of the queue, slowly, slowly, no more than 20 miles an hour. Eventually we got within sight of flashing blue lights.

'Can you crack your window six inches?' I said.

Behind me, the tinted window rolled down slightly.

A copper came straight over and I jerked my thumb behind me. He looked at RS. The copper went over to the car to the front and right of us.

'You, reverse back there,' he said, so they did as they were told.

We pulled out in front and I found the motorway completely empty. So you couldn't always say that there wasn't a separate set of rules for the rich and famous.

But for the police, it's often better to get someone well known out of a situation like that than to risk encouraging the public to pile out of their motors and have a look, so causing even more delays and congestion.

But the UK bodyguards still couldn't get away with half what their American counterparts were used to doing over there and that's why that American singer I walked down on the Brits boat employed me as her security for the next few days.

She came over to the UK so frequently that she had bought a penthouse apartment for when she stayed in town. Strangely, it was in a distinctly unglamorous part of east London: Tower Hamlets. I took her to appear on *Parkinson* and then to a showcase gig to promote her new album.

We got her back safely and, as we got in the lift that served her apartment, my colleague Lloydy and I stood behind her. I became aware that he was staring intently at the back of her neck. Even before he'd started to reach up to her ear, I knew he was going to do it – call it bodyguard intuition. I slapped his hand down.

'Don't,' I muttered.

'What?'

'*Don't!*'

Luckily, she didn't notice. *Thank God!*

We said our goodbyes and I waited until Lloydy and I were safely in the lift again before I said anything.

'What was that all about?' I asked, still shocked enough at the breach of etiquette to continue hissing out of the corner of my mouth, even though there was no way we could be overheard.

'She had a bit of fluff below her ear.'

'That wasn't fluff,' I muttered. 'That was a *stitch*!'

A bodyguard shouldn't touch their client anyway, not unless they are in physical danger. And you certainly don't touch their face, particularly not in her case. She'd had a lot of surgery. Who knows what might have happened if he'd pulled her stitch out? She could have unravelled.

CHAPTER 16

BURGER BAR OF THE STARS

It's a short bus ride from Hyde Park to Frith Street. An ordinary red, London double-decker, a handful of bored, early-evening passengers, grubby seats, a preoccupied conductor and Bruce the legend. He's sitting next to me. That trademark smirk is even wider than usual. Nobody has noticed him because nobody expects him to be there. It's been a long time since Bruce has been invisible and he's loving it!

The conductor rings out our tickets and hands over change. Jolted from his thoughts, he does a double-take.

'Gawd,' he says to Bruce. 'You look just like him!'

That's it. Bruce just cracks up. Suddenly people start to look over our way. Too late because by then it's our stop and we're off, laughing like kids.

'You know, man?' Bruce chuckles, as he steps onto the pavement outside the legendary jazz club Ronnie Scott's. 'You are one crafty motherfucker!'

'Who's going to believe you were on the bus?' I ask him. 'This is the way to do it! If people don't want to believe, they're not going to believe it. They'll tell themselves you're a lookalike.'

The coat check boy is just as stunned to see the club's special guest as anyone on the bus. You know when they say someone's mouth 'hangs open' in surprise? Well, that's exactly what this lad does. His jaw actually drops. Cool as a cucumber, Bruce leans over the desk and gently closes the lad's gob for him.

'I'll see you on the way out, kid,' he drawls, as he strolls into the venue.

And we have a great night – though he calls me 'Bro' all the time. He's been doing this ever since he arrived in the UK. I still can't work out why. In the end, I just have to ask.

'Man, when I come to England I got my bro – I'm coming for my bro,' he says. I think this is lovely. He wants everyone to feel comfortable, not to feel in awe of him.

Though I think it's good of him to do this, there's never any danger of me being in awe of anyone. I don't care how famous or rich they are, they're just doing a job and so am I. I never let myself get drawn into their world – I know it isn't mine. Do I travel round the world by private jet? No. When I get home, the missus will probably be waiting to say, 'Oi, fatty, do the washing up.' As long as I remember where my place is, I will be okay. Then we can all get on together.

The cloakroom attendant is still at his post when we leave that night. He is reading a book and Bruce asks him what it is.

'Oh, I'm studying,' he stammers, looking nervous all over again. Without being asked, Bruce signs the book for him.

'*Jesus!* Thanks!' says the lad, 'Thanks a lot!'

As we head back to the hotel, Bruce says, 'Simple things like that mean such a lot. That's why I can't understand some of my crowd when they forget that and act like arseholes, 'cos that's as easy as it is.'

The journey that would end in the laidback company of Bruce had started with me in the Bon Bonne, in its very last week of business.

That was when Johnny turned up.

A mate from the old days, he was very big in the bodyguard world and he'd been doing very well. He gave me a big hug.

'Cor, you look well, son!' he said. 'Fuck me, you do look well!'

I was so pleased that at last someone could say that to me. It reinforced my feeling that I was really on my way. And things only got better. Later in the evening, he told me that he needed some force on the ground for a launch.

'It's going to be a chain of restaurants,' he explained, 'owned by three of the biggest movie stars in the world.'

'Bloody hell!' I said. 'Who?'

It was three huge American Hollywood stars. What were they doing, getting into the restaurant game? I presumed they needed something for the pension fund just like anyone else. It didn't bother me, anyway – I just thought having names like that on my CV would be absolutely brilliant for business.

'Yeah, I'm definitely up for that, mate,' I told Johnny. Silently, I offered up a little prayer of thanks to God that I had taken up the invite to do the last few days at the Bon Bonne.

Every last detail of that launch was booked up months in advance, but it wasn't until relatively close to the time that I discussed the logistics with Johnny. When the day came, I found myself looking forward to the graft with the stars – getting myself back to where I felt I belonged among the elite. But when I got to Johnny's office I was disappointed to see that I was right at the back of the running order. My excitement faded into disappointment. I wanted to be up there with the boys themselves, doing the close protection, but I was going to be miles away.

I asked if my expertise wasn't better deployed nearer to the action.

'That's the position we've got open,' said Johnny abruptly. I think he was trying me out, seeing how I did before letting me back into frontline work. Anyway, there was no way that I was going to turn this down – it was too good an opportunity to miss.

'I'll do it,' I said.

So I ended up in the back vehicle. The other fellas took their positions in the lead and we made up a box formation. There was getting on for 20 bodyguards in all. Three stars of that calibre required nothing less.

We did the transfer from the airport to the hotel and it all went very well, as did the first day. The big opening was to be the following night, giving us a chance to go over the logistics once again during the day and double-check everything. It all had to run to the second, from the hotel to the venue and the return journey.

Everything went like clockwork. And it was a good job that it did – the crowd those legends pulled was massive. Thousands turned out to greet their heroes in the West End, the screaming and the shouting was deafening.

The three stars were absolutely lovely. They played up to the crowd like the troupers they were, giving everyone a great wave. Then they cut the ribbon and we were inside, surrounded by the memorabilia they'd donated themselves to decorate the restaurant.

A similar routine followed the next night, when we took

all of them to appear together on the *Parkinson* show. We got them to the studios, they did the show and everything went well. Before they left, they wanted to say thank you to us. It was the first time I had an inkling I must have been doing something right.

The boys said to us all, 'Well done, guys, you made us feel very safe. We wouldn't have done it without you. We're really pleased.'

Then Bruce came up to me personally and said, 'Listen, I've seen what you've done and don't think I haven't – I really feel safe around you. Next time I'm in town, maybe we should get together.'

'That would be great,' I said, 'if you want. It would be entirely up to you.'

I didn't want to overstep the mark because I was always aware that I was working for Johnny. There was no way that I was going to give even an impression of wanting to take his clients from him, but Bruce's office did make that call in the end.

'Hi!' said this bright voice. 'Is that Roy?'

'Well... yes,' I said. It had been so long since the launch that I'd forgotten all about it.

'Hi! This is Cindy. I'm calling on behalf of one of my artists. He'll be arriving tomorrow and he would like to have your assistance. It's Bruce. He's asked for you specifically.'

Well, bloody hell! That says something, I thought. *He was a man of his word. I must have made an impression after all.*

I got the running order for the trip from Cindy. Bruce was over for a movie première. He was going to be around for a few days doing press in the UK and he would be staying at the Hyde Park Hotel.

As soon as he arrived, we fast-tracked him through arrivals and he smiled in recognition when he saw me waiting for him.

'Hi, bro!' he said. 'Nice to see you again! I told you I'd come back with you.'

He had a couple of days to fill before the première and I didn't mind spending it with him – he was a pleasure to be around. You wouldn't have thought he was a Hollywood superstar: he was laidback and down-to-earth, a genuine, nice fella.

We got chatting and that was when I first found out that he was so into jazz. Any form of it, he really loved it. And he didn't have a bad voice himself – he could throw a tune, though I did once jokingly tell him, 'Stick to yer acting!'

All the press calls for the movie were taken inside the hotel. Each journalist would get a few minutes and then the PR would usher in another one. It was just a production line. After a day or so of that, I could tell he was knackered. He'd barely been able to get out of his room, much less have a proper break.

My guess was right. Later that afternoon he called through to my company office.

'I can't stay here another night, bro,' said a despairing Bruce. 'I've got nothing planned, it's driving me mad. I just need to get out.'

That was when I hatched my little scheme: take him to Ronnie Scott's in Mayfair. It was a quiet Wednesday, we could do it without having to use a massive entourage. I decided to create the ultimate anti-disguise disguise. Leave the trademark cap and shades at the hotel – too obvious. It might work for another star, but it was exactly that outfit which everyone knew him for. He wore a shirt, jeans and shoes rather than the trainers. I wore the same sort of gear. Casual. Around 9.30pm we made our way down to the lobby of the Hyde Park Hotel and out onto the street. And Bruce was looking. Left, right, I could tell what he was thinking – where's the limo?

So I told him what his mode of transport was going to be for that evening.

And he looked at me. 'You shitting me, bro?' he asked.

'No, I'm not shitting you,' I told him, adding, 'Don't say anything, just sit on the bus – it's only five stops up the road. You'll get far less attention this way, believe me.'

But I could tell he wasn't convinced. However, he ended up having an amazing time and getting to sample a bit of the normality that most of us take for granted.

The following night's première went off really well. I did the walk-down with Bruce and the crowd was phenomenal.

I wondered how many of the fans knew that the stars never actually stayed for the entire movie. In fact, they don't watch any of it – they've made the bloody thing, they've probably seen it a dozen times already. The cast, director and key crew give a speech on a stage in front of the screen, have a little chuckle, blah, blah, blah, and as soon as the lights go down... *Bang, we're off out the side door, in the car and gone! See you at the afterparty.*

When Bruce finally got ready to fly home, he promised to stay in touch – and he did. He said he'd always ask for me when he was town. Then he gave me a hug and said, 'You're genuine, I feel safe and you know what you're doing. That's all I can ever ask from anyone.'

As I drove home that night, I thought, *God, that's probably one of the nicest things any client has ever said to me.* And I knew what it meant – it meant a lot for the business, too. When someone like Bruce says that kind of thing, you've got a ticket to America, which is good for anywhere. I knew the word would soon get round.

CHAPTER 17
PAULA YATES

It had been a quiet day when Martin Kemp called. I knew, of course, that Paula Yates, the ex-wife of Bob Geldof, had died the previous week – 17 September 2000. You couldn't not know – the papers had been full of it for days.

Knowing us through the PAs we did for *EastEnders*, Martin wanted us to take him to her funeral. Paula was such a well-loved figure and it was still amazing to see how many turned up. I'd met her once when she was doing Channel 4's *The Tube*, a really nice lady. I never dreamed at the time that she had the problems that led to her death, but I guess some people can hide it well. I knew myself that drugs can be tucked away. Even what I call the 'big one', the 'big H', you can hide it from the best of them.

'Yeah, that's no problem, Martin,' I said. It was just Ronnie and me who took him.

''Ere, 'ave a look!' gasped Ronnie when we got to the graveyard.

'*What?*'

'Look, over there!'

There was only a guy on a step ladder up against the wall of the cemetery. He was leaning over the wall with a telescopic lens pointed at the mourners. Paparazzo. At a funeral!

Come on – have a bit of respect!

'Unbelievable,' sighed Ronnie. 'They're like animals, ain't they?' And he was right.

We kept going round the block and the guy on the gate, who recognised me from the circuit, waved us through.

'Nice to have you here, Roy,' he called out. 'I feel much better already!'

We followed a little road to a church in the cemetery and pulled over on the right, where there were a few other cars parked up. Martin made his way to join the other friends and family.

Now we could see the front of the photographer as he squinted over the wall through his lens. He had positioned himself directly above a freshly-dug, open grave. I assumed he was guessing that was where Paula Yates was going to be buried. Not that he was to know, but she would be taken elsewhere to be cremated. Anyway, that wasn't the point. For God's sake, how could he be so disrespectful as to try and get a picture of a coffin being lowered into the ground?

'I can't have that!' I growled to Ronnie. We jumped back in the car and drove out slowly. Bono and The Edge from U2, both of whom I'd worked with, were coming the other way. I smiled and said hello, while simultaneously beginning to think of a plan.

I got Ronnie to hang a left and we cruised slowly round the block until we were passing that muppet with his camera. He was still on the steps and I was in the passenger seat on the side of the car nearest him.

'What you gonna do?' asked Ronnie, suspiciously.

'Just keep going,' I told him. 'When you get near him, slow down.'

'Don't start your bollocks, Snell!' he said. 'Not here!'

'No,' I said reassuringly. 'Of course not.'

As he slowed down, I reached out and grabbed the steps.

'Off you go, Ron!'

Screech! Ronnie took off and the geezer went *flying!*

I glanced in the wing mirror and saw him sprawled by the wall, his camera in pieces on the road. He looked in our direction and he wasn't best pleased, but nor would he be taking more photographs of graves.

I felt I'd done a little something for the family on what was a terrible day for them. However, I don't think Bob Geldof ever knew about it, but that wasn't the point for me. I just thought they deserved a bit of respect.

We got back to the church in time for the service. The people who spoke were phenomenal. I won't say any more about it, because it was a private matter and it should really stay with Geldof and his family.

CHAPTER 18

A FAREWELL TO FRANK

I'd been doing her security for a while when Diana, the Queen of Motown, did the Royal Variety Performance in 2001. At the end of the gig, she held up a hand in the middle of the applause.

'I'd just like to say thank you to a certain guy, because you know, without him I wouldn't be here tonight. And deep down, I love him so much because he makes me feel so safe. I would like to call him out here...

'Roy? Would you come out here? Come on, honey – I know you're shy, but I want you out here. Guess I'm gonna need a little help here, ladies and gentlemen.'

Fuck! Was that *my* name? Did I just hear my name? She was talking to me. *Fucking hell, turn it in, love!* Then the spotlight was turned on me. *Boom!* And all I could think was that I was working and I didn't want it to be happening.

She got all 5,000 people in the venue to chant my name and suddenly the hairs on the back of my neck stood up and I thought, *Bloody hell! Now I know how* they *feel.* And all I could hear was: 'Roy! Roy! Roy!'

Diana laughed and I really thought I was going to kill her.

'Are you going to come out?' she teased. 'Or do I have to come and get you, honey?'

It didn't leave me much choice.

I stepped out onto the stage and as I did so, the whole place went mad. My legs felt like lead and I wagged a finger at her, sort of telling her off. Then she beckoned me towards her and put her arms around me. She kissed me on the cheek and said, 'He's all mine! Thank you, Roy. Ladies and gentlemen, I've never felt so safe – this guy is the *best*!'

She dedicated her next song to me – 'Ain't No Mountain High Enough'.

I shuffled about with her for a bit, then whispered in her ear, 'Listen, I've really go to go and do my job.' I was crapping myself.

'Please, give it up for Mister Roy!' she called. As I gawped at her, she said, 'Here, these are for you.' And from nowhere appeared this beautiful big bouquet of flowers. I thanked her and stumbled off the stage. Someone from her entourage was waiting and they took the flowers from me to keep them safe until the end of the night.

Ol' Blue Eyes' farewell gig at the Royal Albert Hall was emotional for very different reasons, though. He'd had quite a few 'last' tours, but everyone knew this really was it. It put me in a unique position because until then he'd always had a very tight team around him, but the law had changed and foreign bodyguards had to be accompanied by English colleagues in the UK. The final straw had been Madonna's Blonde Ambition tour. She'd been out jogging in Hyde Park surrounded by her entourage. A sixteen-year-old girl tried to get the singer's autograph and one of Madonna's bodyguards broke the kid's nose. *What a way to behave!* He just put his hand out and *bosh*, that was it.

I've never seen any need for that sort of thing. As far as I'm concerned, you need to get people on side. And I don't just mean the fans: if you're polite to everyone from the hotel manager to the staff who make the beds, they'll become your eyes and ears when you're not around.

Ol' Blue Eyes turned up at the venue hours late. He was quite a big guy. Less alert than I thought he would be, quite tired after the journey and also extraordinarily serious in his manner. But he still had the attitude about him – and those piercing eyes.

He shook my hand and said, 'Hi.'

'Lovely to meet you,' I said. 'It's an honour, I have to say.'

'That's very kind of you,' he replied. 'I hear you're working for us here?'

'Yes, certainly – I'll make sure everything will be done for you.'

'Thank you very much... I'm sure it will be a great evening.'

He stayed in his dressing room until it was time for him to take to the stage. And it just felt like he'd changed somehow. The weariness from travelling, the awkwardness of age... it all fell away. You could feel his eagerness to get back on stage; he couldn't wait, that was it for him. That's where he felt at home, where he wanted to be.

For him, everything else was just waiting, waiting for the moment. And I guessed that wasn't something that came easily to Frank. I reckon he'd have parked the plane next to the Albert Hall if he could and walked straight down the steps and up to the microphone.

I watched as he walked from the corridor behind the stage up the stairs. The lights came on and the roar from the crowd was like nothing I'd ever heard before. And that was before he'd even opened his mouth – all he'd done was smile. They went absolutely nuts at him; it was all about presence.

And, if I'm being completely honest, his performance didn't quite match it. Halfway through the opening number, he seemed to need a bit of help. I suppose this could have been for effect, but I got the impression he was struggling to remember the words. But he didn't need to worry because the audience were singing it for him. He'd only need to point the mic towards them and they'd fill in for him. His style was effortless.

He did two encores and then I got him into the dressing room. I'd been right about him not liking to hang about. He was changed and out within 20 minutes, still wearing a sort of towelling scarf that he'd wrapped round his neck to keep his throat warm.

'Thanks very much,' he politely told me, but now that he was away from the stage, his manner was serious as it had been before. 'Really appreciate your help. Best of luck for the future.'

His guys whisked him down the corridor and I got him out of the stage door. His limo was parked virtually inside the building and they had him out and away in seconds; they didn't even wait for his security men who'd been with me. There were other guys inside the car and they shut the door before he'd even sat back in his seat. It was fast.

But that really was a farewell. It had been his last-ever performance in the UK.

CHAPTER 19

STABBED IN STREATHAM

I glanced down at my chest and saw the handle sticking out of me. *Oh... shit!* Without a second thought, I pushed the artist towards the car and threw them into the back seat – there was no time for ceremony. Turning back, I dealt with the attacker fast and ferociously. He was in a pretty poor state, to say the least, when I'd finished with him. I was more concerned about myself, about the blade. The key was to stay calm.

Staff poured out of the venue and the alleyway was filled with noise, activity and panic. But I knew that it would be a fatal move – literally – to allow myself to become excited. My heart needed to be working slowly, not pumping blood round like crazy when I had a bloody great knife sticking in me. And yet I couldn't risk pulling the damn thing out. The blade was the only thing that was preventing claret from spurting all over the shop. *Keep it in there!* Fuck me, it didn't half hurt. Fit as I was, this was agony.

I moved swiftly, but stayed in control: I sat myself down in the passenger seat and hoped the police wouldn't stop me for not wearing my seatbelt. Under the circumstances, it was kind of difficult to get it on.

'King's College,' I said to Steve, the driver. It was the hospital in nearby Camberwell.

When I was last injured in the line of duty I had sorted it out myself, but that was when I was coked-up monster who thought he was invincible even when he was shot. At that time I had every reason not to get the authorities involved, but now I was protecting a famous client and everything must be done on the level. Besides, it was one thing to have a bullet lodged out of the way at the bottom of your leg, but this was a blade way up in my chest and it might do even more damage – maybe it had already. I was old enough to know better now: I wasn't going to wait for the ambulance... or try DIY surgery.

My passenger was getting increasingly agitated.

'You keep calm and all,' I said. It helped to feel I was in control. At King's, I carefully got out of the car.

'Take off,' I instructed Steve.

'I want to stay...' pleaded the singer.

'You are *not*,' I replied. '*Get away!*'

Reception was staffed by a woman looking like what I'm old-fashioned enough to call a matron – blue uniform, important air about her, very busy. *Too busy to look up!*

'Yes, be with you in a minute,' she called, still scribbling away. If I wasn't in such screaming pain, I might have laughed.

'I was wondering if you might help me...' I began, still keeping myself calm. It took every ounce of my training, but I managed not to give in.

With perfect comic timing, she said, 'And what seems to be the problem?' before looking up. The 'problem' was now at her eye-level.

'Oh my *God!*' she exclaimed.

'Yes,' I said lightly, nodding down at the handle. 'That *is* the problem.'

In the cubicle, a doctor sized me up coolly. With my top off, he could see that the blade was right up by my nipple. He looked at my face and down at the wound then back up again.

'You'll probably never see this again in your career,' he remarked to his colleague. 'Look at the wound. Can you explain that?' The other man shook his head in amazement. It was bleeding, but not nearly to the extent that you'd expect following that kind of attack. He addressed me again. 'How long have you had it slowed down?' He meant the heartbeat – he knew exactly the technique I had been taught for situations like this.

I glanced at my watch. 'Twenty-three minutes,' I said.

It all seemed so much longer ago...

As a bodyguard, you never know when you're going to get in trouble, but that's all part of the job. Even so, when I agreed to help out a colleague who'd been let down, I had no idea that I would end up being stabbed in return.

The artist in question was to perform a comeback showcase at a venue in Streatham in front of up to 400 people, including important record company suits. I don't want to give away any details about this particular singer; I don't think it's fair. It wouldn't be respectful. Let's just say this was a very controversial person in their time and leave it at that. Just call them... *the singer*.

But what I will say is that for all the fuss that was made about this singer, this was a really lovely person once you got to meet them. They had a reputation for not suffering fools gladly and for speaking from the heart, which often got them in trouble. But they didn't take themselves or the business too seriously, as I found out. We hit it off as soon as we met at the airport.

'Roy, are you hungry?' was almost the first question.

'Yeah, I am, as it happens,' I replied.

'Me too, I'm starving. Let's go to McDonald's.'

'Do *what*?' I said incredulously. 'We're *not* going to take *you* into McDonald's! Are you having a laugh?' They'd be mobbed straightaway. 'Tell you what,' I compromised. 'Let's go to the drive-in.' There, we scoffed a Big Mac each and then I got the singer off to their hotel and settled in. Lovely.

The gig was the following night and the singer still didn't want any fuss to be made about their appearance. In and out, that was the idea.

The gig itself went off very well. There were no problems at the soundcheck; I checked out all the entrances and exits, and made sure everything was secure – all very routine. The set had some great new material. I got the impression that the singer was very pleased with the way it went. They were in a very jovial mood afterwards; things were looking good.

About 15 minutes before we were due to leave, I asked Steve to bring the car round to the side entrance of the venue, a less-than-glamorous exit. You opened the door straight onto a grubby alley, where they kept the wheelie bins.

I went out first to check there was no trouble and that the car was waiting so the singer could be whisked away without any delay. It was then that I heard a faint noise, which seemed to be coming from the other side of the big bins. I couldn't exactly identify what it was, but I knew enough to trust my instincts and my training – and everything was telling me that something was up.

No time to hang around. I shoved the bin against the wall – not an elegant solution, but if anyone happened to be lurking behind the rubbish, they would end up squashed against the far side of the alley with a serious headache.

I was right about the noise, but the acoustics in the alleyway were deceptive. Trouble was hiding behind the door I'd just opened, not behind the bins. I hadn't given the all clear for the singer to come through and they knew the drill – stay back until I said to come out.

Or at least... they *should* have known.

Perhaps they did or maybe they forgot. They might just have been being their usual headstrong self and didn't want to wait. I didn't have time to find out because the singer marched out... straight into the line of danger.

A bloke pushed from behind the door and I saw a glint in his hand, just a glint. Immediately, I went into automatic pilot. I didn't have a chance to do anything more than throw myself between him and the singer; it all happened so quickly. That second, I felt a sharp pain as the knife slid in.

The doctor's diagnosis was that the blade hadn't penetrated far. He didn't think it was that long a weapon; the handle was likely to be longer. It seemed I'd been lucky. Did that mean the attacker hadn't intended to do serious harm? I didn't know. You could do plenty of damage with something that size if you struck the artery feeding the neck.

Was it premeditated or just a random crackpot? Hard to say. I remembered the singer themselves had said to me on the way to the venue that they seemed to attract more than their fair share of cranks. Someone had even sent them a letter written in their own blood.

Gently, but smartly, the doctor pulled the blade out. There

was hardly any blood flow. He swabbed the wound, cleaned what was left of the nipple and stapled me up, *bosh*!

'There you go,' he said. 'The good news is that's okay now. The bad news is... you've only got half a tit.'

I hung around for more than 90 minutes, waiting for the police to arrive. My mind was racing, thinking about the statement I would have to make. But nothing happened. The hospital staff moved me out to the corridor, I was all ready to go and still nothing. *Bloody hell! Sod this!* So I jumped in a taxi and went back to the hotel to check on the singer. They were still very worried about me.

'Don't be dramatic,' I said. 'It's fine. As far as I'm concerned, it was over before it started. Let's not get carried away here.' The singer and I parted on good terms, reassured that each of us was fine.

I voluntarily went to the local Streatham nick; I knew I'd dealt with the attacker severely and I expected some kind of comeback. But the coppers told me there would be no charges. It suited me fine; I didn't want to pursue it either. As far as I was concerned, it was all part of the job. It's too easy to get wrapped up in those things. There's the press, you get called a hero, all that... But I just did what I had to do.

And now I had a stab wound to add to my bullet wound and all the teeth I've had knocked out and the pummelling I've taken over the years. They say being a bodyguard is such a glamorous life – well, it doesn't half hurt sometimes, I can tell you!

The following week, the stitches came out and my poor body made an amazingly quick recovery. I was soon back at the graft, though to this day I've still only got half a tit!

CHAPTER 20

WHEN EDEN ARRIVED

Joanne announced she was pregnant in 1997, but things rarely seem to go smoothly with me and this was no exception. She missed the due date and eventually the hospital decided to induce the birth.

They told me it was going to be a breech birth – the head wasn't engaging. Joanne was in a terrible state, she really was getting herself in a right tizzy; anything would set her off. Her sister Diane was supporting her but it was incredibly difficult for all of us, just waiting. The doctors had tried everything and her blood pressure was going through the roof.

Diane went home as their mother, Anne, arrived. Joanne was acting quite strangely, so I called for assistance. I couldn't say exactly what it was, but something didn't seem quite right to me.

The nurse came in to check the monitors and equipment. There was a weird bleeping sound; it definitely didn't sound right to me. The surgeon came in and checked and double-checked while I hovered anxiously.

'We need to get her into theatre,' he confirmed. 'Straight away. Mr Snell, gown up.'

What did he say? I was going in – after they made me sign a waiver to say that if I passed out, I wouldn't sue the hospital. I wondered to myself if they knew who they were asking – I'd seen more than my fair share of blood and guts. At least, that's what I thought. But this was my own family. I might not have been able to admit it even to myself, but I was close to falling apart.

I was trying to make light of everything and to appear not too concerned, but deep down, I knew that something serious was happening. The staff seemed very reluctant to say what was going on and that did nothing to reassure me. It was only afterwards that I found out.

The truth was as simple as it was horrifying: Joanne's heart had stopped and so had the baby's.

We were rushed to theatre and, as the anaesthetist leaned over her and gave her whatever it was she needed to make her better, I received a sign that maybe everything was going to be okay, after all. Joanne squeezed my hand and opened her eyes. She focused weakly on me and whispered to me.

'Cor,' she hissed, 'he's got *such* bad breath...' That was my Joanne all over! The wife I loved so much was well and truly back.

Now they needed to carry out an emergency caesarean – and fast. The surgeon set about it as if he were in a race. It seemed to me that he had her opened up in under two minutes. Even then it was going to be some battle.

'This baby,' he said, 'does *not* want to come out.'

At last they got them out of immediate danger, though Joanne was still barely conscious. I didn't understand half of what was going on.

'Congratulations,' the surgeon said, after what seemed like hours. 'You have a little daughter.' What a tiny bundle! No noise, though. No crying. They kept wiping her and tapping her. I couldn't stand it.

For God's sake! Just let me hear her cry. For God's sake!

Joanne was back with us by then, as tense as I was. The moments stretched on. And then it seemed like a tiny motor had started up – it was our daughter, her lungs whirring into motion at last. *She's started to cry!*

My laughter sounded close to tears... hysteria.

They took her away to weigh her and check her out while they put Joanne back together again. She had all these tubes sticking out of her and she had gone out again. It wasn't until she'd been wheeled almost all the way back to her spot in the ward that she properly regained consciousness.

I said, 'You didn't half put me through a lot there!'

'Are we going in the garden?' she asked faintly.

'Do *what*?' I asked. I wondered if she was still not quite all there.

'Are we going in the garden?' she repeated. 'I need a fag!'

'No, you *can't* go in the bloody garden for a bleedin' fag!' I laughed.

She gave a grumpy little moan of disappointment, bless her heart. We discussed what had just happened.

'How was it?' I asked. I still didn't really know what she had been through.

'It just felt like I was going,' she admitted. 'All of a sudden it felt like I was in the Garden of Eden.' And there was our daughter's name. Right there: Eden. It couldn't be anything else. Eden Lauren, born 21 June 1998 – Father's Day. It couldn't have been any more perfect, even though she took her time getting there.

Mother and daughter had to stay in the hospital for another few days before I was finally allowed to take them home. We'd spent a fortune getting the nursery just right and although the household changed forever, it was for the better. Best thing that ever happened to us, to me.

But it wasn't long before I had to return to reality and get back to work. We were just getting into doing the rockers, the old school rock'n'roll. And you didn't get much more rock'n'roll than the Rock Awards.

The ceremony was held at the Hammersmith Odeon. I met Rod for the first time that night and I'd get to know him a lot better later. Mick and Ronnie were also there. One of my jobs was to make sure they weren't bothered by people wanting autographs. None of that lot really liked to give them out and Mick in particular was well known for very rarely signing his name. I also had to escort the stars to the loo – their own superstar toilet.

The awards went very well and the special guests had a great time. At the end of the night, I took them to their limos and that was the start of my relationship with rock aristocracy. I did shock rocker Marilyn Manson. I called him by his real name, Brian, and although Manson might scare the shit out of you with all that make-up, he proved to be quite a nice fella underneath it all. Slipknot was another bunch of hard rockers who looked even more bizarre than Brian ever did.

I'd come home after I'd been doing artists like that and Joanne wouldn't have much more idea than me who it was that I'd just been working with. But I couldn't be choosy about who I took on, not now that I had a baby to support. And I did get to meet a completely different style of fan through bands like that. You'd walk out with the artists and be surrounded by all these kids who looked like

Frankenstein's monster and Dracula. Then there'd be a bunch of people wearing masks that made them look like they'd got disfigured faces. It was pretty chaotic, pretty weird.

Bryan Adams was far more mainstream, a Canadian with a home in London. My first job with him was an airport transfer. They said he was very down-to-earth and wouldn't be having any of the VIP treatment at the airport. I thought that was bloody lovely, to be honest. He just came through like everyone else rather than being taken out of a side entrance like those who like to call themselves A-listers.

I'm going to get on with this guy, I thought. *He's not got his head stuck up his arse.*

Sometimes I stood at the airport with my client's name on a board, but I hardly thought I needed to do that with Bryan Adams.

Really?

Time passed and it seemed as if everyone was coming off the plane except him. I'd checked the arrivals beforehand and so I knew the flight hadn't been delayed. And after a while everyone *had* come off the plane and there was still no sign of him. I convinced myself that he'd got stuck in customs.

I turned away and saw a bloke in the corner with a little suitcase – and he'd got the raving hump! You could see it in his face. He'd glance down at his watch and then look around. Poor bastard, he'd been standing over there almost as long as I'd been stood about ten yards away from him.

'Excuse me,' I said, as I moved over to him smartly. 'You're Bryan?'

'Yes,' he interrupted. 'Where have you been?'

'I've been standing over there!'

'Well, I've been here for 40 minutes.'

'Oh, well, there's no point in arguing about it,' I said cheekily. 'Just get in the motor, I'll take you home, son. Don't worry about it. Roysie's here, I'll take care of ya.'

He must have thought, who is this nutter?

I got him settled in the car and headed back towards town.

'How was your flight, then?'

'Better than the pick-up!'

'You're never going to forgive me for that,' I told him. 'You go on like a bleedin' old woman, you do! We've got a long drive home, let's start again. My name is Roy Snell and you're Bryan Adams. Is that correct?'

I glanced back in the mirror and saw the beginnings of a smirk on his face.

'Yeah, okay then, Roy,' he said, beginning to relax. We just clicked after that and two days later, he called me to take him around and I worked with him loads. I was there to sympathise when he had a burglary and we got chatting about security, and I was all ready to advise him on how he might upgrade.

'I've got a better idea,' he said. 'I'll take your photo.'

I had no idea what he was going on about.

'Nah, I don't do all that,' I said. 'I don't do pictures.'

I need to be anonymous to do my job and I don't want to become part of that world. The last thing I need is to find myself splattered all over some newspaper or other. But what I didn't realise was that Bryan Adams was an accomplished photographer and he'd had quite a bit of work exhibited. He was damn good at it.

'You don't understand,' he said, 'I just want you to hold these.'

He passed me two bits of brass tubing, saying 'Just look mean.'

'I already look mean,' I told him. 'How can I look meaner?'

Then I scowled at him.

'That's it,' he said. 'That's the one! Get angry, give me the angry look.'

He started laughing.

'You mean *this one*?' I growled. I pointed the tubes at him and it looked like I was shoving a sawn-off in his face. He started snapping away, still laughing.

'Happy now?' I asked.

'Can't wait,' he said. 'I'm going to have that etched into the glass of my front and back door. And underneath I'm going to inscribe, "Please come in. My friend wants to meet you".'

And he did. So if those burglars ever came back, they'd see my beautiful face warning them off...

Bryan was a bit of a daredevil and almost killed himself on holiday in Thailand. He took a motorbike up some narrow hill roads and managed to drive himself off the side of a cliff. By rights, that should have been it, except that he landed in a tree about a hundred foot down. The bike tumbled down to the bottom and left him dangling. He told me all about it as I drove him to his alternative doctor in Chiswick.

'I held on, and kept shouting and shouting for help,' he said.

'How long for?'

'Nine hours.'

Nine hours? Poor bastard, he was stuck there all day. Eventually someone found him and they rushed him to hospital and checked him over. He was pretty banged up – more bruised than broken, but it still hurt like fuck.

We got him to the herbal doctor and I helped him hobble

in. I waited for him in the car – it gave me a chance to have a quick salmon. I guess he was in there for something like ninety minutes. But the Bryan Adams who came out was completely different: he was skipping to the car. I was a bit of a cynic about the whole alternative thing, but I have to say it seemed to have worked. *Acupuncture!*

I worked with Bryan for a year or so and we got to know one another properly. He asked me to do the security for his 40th birthday party. I've already written a bit about that in the introduction to this book, but I didn't mention that he had a surprise guest at his birthday. In fact, Bryan's friends had given me the job of organising the whole thing without him knowing.

Talk about headache! The logistics of keeping it out of the press were nightmarish. And it was a *very* special guest. You have to understand that even the stars have their own idols. Melanie Chisholm of the Spice Girls *loved* Bryan Adams, that's why they did a record together. Well, to be honest, I think he half-fancied her, though he didn't really have a chance!

It was one of his assistants who told me who Bryan's idol was.

'Look,' he said, 'He's one of the biggest fans in the world of Barry, the Walrus of Love.'

You wouldn't have thought it of someone like Bryan Adams, him being a rocker.

Barry flew under a pseudonym on a private jet that landed at a tiny airport in Farnborough, well away from any of the major hubs. That meant there were fewer people around to spot him. My car was on the tarmac to meet him and the customs had already been done airside. Barry just came down the steps and straight into the car – *gone*. We drove him into the car park under his hotel, he took the lift directly to his own suite and he didn't go to the lobby to check in. It was a lot of hard work, but I can tell you there wasn't a sausage in the press, not a thing! I was very proud of myself for pulling that one off.

It got to the night of the party and I watched the caterers bringing in the supplies and I realised with horror that all the food there that night was all vegan. What I call 'turtle food' – pumpkins, tofu, vegan cheese...

'Oh, Roy!' said Bryan, when he saw my face. 'I forgot about you! What are we going to do?'

'Don't worry, son,' I said, trying to make him feel better. 'I'll take meself up the kebab shop and get meself a nice greasy...' I didn't even finish my sentence. As soon as I'd got to the word 'kebab', Bryan actually choked. He almost threw up on the spot.

'*Please!*' he cried. 'Don't bring that into my house!'

'A kebab?' *Choke!* 'Nah, it's okay,' I said, 'I'll eat it outside.'

'Can you go down the road a bit?' He couldn't even cope with the concept of the meat being outside his front door. 'I don't want the smell drifting in.'

'Turn it in! I've gotta eat!'

'Yeah, I'm not saying that, just... not in front of the house. Your boys will be all right for a few minutes, just... please... go down there and eat it. On the corner, please.'

Fucking cheek! But he didn't realise that I couldn't be gone for long: I needed to get his special birthday guest in. It was all done to a very tight schedule.

All the other party-goers arrived and Barry was going to come along much later, once everyone had a chance to relax and get into it. I picked him up from the hotel later in the evening – after I'd sneaked my kebab – and drove him back to the house. There, I gave the security knock that my firm used so the boys knew it was me and we smuggled the singer through a side door in the house.

Nervously, I wondered if the birthday boy might not catch a glimpse of him but one bit of luck was that the party was happening in the upper part of the house, which you could only reach via a spiral staircase. One of my guys was posted at the top, another at the bottom. If Bryan unexpectedly decided to go down for any reason, they were to give him some excuse, hold him off. But he was perfectly happy with his mates all night and he didn't suspect a thing.

Barry had time to get changed in a downstairs bedroom and then, just before half-midnight, the DJ made an announcement, as planned.

'We want to wish you a happy birthday, Bryan!' That was the cue to get into position. 'We all hope you have a great time and I know how much you like Barry, so this one is for you.'

Drifting downstairs we could hear, 'You're the First, the Last, My Everything' as I led the way up the spiral staircase, closely followed by the real Barry – and what a moment that was. The man himself, clutching a microphone, waiting to be taken through! Just a few feet away, Bryan was relaxing on his sofa, surrounded by friends, enjoying the music, singing along happily and blissfully unaware of what was heading his way. He didn't have a clue. Not a clue.

I entered the room and did a smart side-step. Barry strode forwards, the DJ slammed on a spotlight and turned down the record a bit. You could hear the unmistakeable rumble, '*You're* my everything,' through the speakers from the genuine article, pointing at Bryan Adams, whose face just crumpled. He couldn't believe it.

He was like a blubber! Tears of joy!

The place erupted, everyone started dancing and Barry played up magnificently. You could tell that he was loving every minute just as much as his stunned super-fan while he performed a superb mini-set of his greatest hits – playing karaoke with himself. Then he and Bryan sat for hours, chatting away like old friends. Bryan couldn't believe that his friends had sorted that out for him.

It all finished about 3.30am and we got everyone back safely – and I still don't think that anyone ever knew that Barry was in the UK that weekend.

At the end of the night, Bryan reserved special thanks for me.

'What can I say?' he began.

'Listen, no problem at all. I'm just so glad you had such a lovely time – if anyone deserves it, you do.'

'Thanks, and I'll need you tomorrow too.'

He was doing a birthday gig of his own – some twenty-one-year-old in Dublin, whose father was one of the richest men in the country and had paid for Bryan to do a personal gig. Three songs. Not only was he paid a fortune but he was also flown there and back by private jet the same night. How spoilt was she!

Bryan later asked me to pick him up at 6am to take him to Heathrow. The job was going to run on after a night working with the chairman of Warner Music. I had to look after this guy while he had a night out at the Hilton in central London and I was a little concerned that I might not have time to get out to Chelsea afterwards, so I called a colleague on the circuit and asked him if he'd cover for me.

'Yeah, no problem, mate,' he said.

It was just an insurance policy. And on the night, my

client came out of the hotel not long after half-midnight and said that he'd be ready to go in about fifteen minutes. Sweet. I figured I could get him back to Sheen, get my head down for four or five hours and still be at Bry's for 6 o'clock.

Oh, yeah? I shouldn't have been so confident.

Almost as soon as he'd gone back in to get ready, I nipped out of the car for my usual quick smoke. As I was standing by the front door, I heard a bit of an argument going on in the foyer, a woman shouting and screaming, closely followed by some bloke.

'Just shut up!' he was shouting. 'You're driving me mad! You're always fucking starting all the fucking time!'

I didn't take much notice of it. Another couple came out and the two women started arguing with each other. I was still waiting for my man as the foursome emerged from the hotel and one of the blokes made the biggest mistake of his life, the biggest. The one thing I will never, *ever* tolerate – and I never have – is a man hitting a woman. My blood just boils. No matter what – a woman can shout at you, she can smack you one, but you don't hit her back. Not in front of Roy Snell.

One of the women had gone after this fella and given him a mighty shove.

'You're a fucking arsehole!' she told him and walked off. That could have been it, or at least it *should* have been it. But he charged after her and *bang!* He punched her in the face while his mate held her. Not even a slap. He punched her. She didn't half hit the ground, out cold.

Then the little shit who did it suddenly became aware of a presence watching him. Silent. Not moving. Me. Now, this geezer was in a lot of trouble all ready, a lot of trouble, whether or not he knew it. And he didn't do himself any favours with his next move.

'*What?*' he asked, glaring at me. 'You got something to say an' all?'

Not really, no, I don't have anything to say.

Bosh!

Spark out on the pavement.

For the first time, the other woman smiled.

'Serves him fucking right,' she said.

With immaculate timing, the chairman of Warner Music appeared and paused to inspect the scene.

'Nothing to do with you, Roysie?' he enquired casually.

'Nothing to do with me, mate!' I said cheerfully, rubbing my right hand down my shirt. 'Shall we go?'

I opened the door for him and we drove away, leaving both parties still unconscious outside the Hilton.

Someone there must have been awake enough to take my number plate, though, because by the time I'd gone to Sheen and as far back towards home as Richmond, thinking it was only just gone one in the morning and I was still doing quite well for time, I was pulled over by the old bill.

Here we go...

One of the officers strolled over to my window.

'Where are you off to, sir?' he asked.

'I'm just about to go home.'

'Where have you been?'

'I've come from... the West End,' I said, trying to avoid being more specific. But I knew what he was asking about and I had to admit it was the Hilton.

'Were you involved in a fracas?' he asked. I tried to deny it and out he came with the usual police jargon they reserve for these sorts of occasions. 'We have had reports of an altercation', 'we have reason to believe...' all that stuff. I was cautioned, though not arrested, and taken to the local police station in Richmond.

Now I was getting a bit nervous. Not so much about the arrest, but the time. I still had to pick up Bryan Adams and I could do without all the aggro.

It wasn't until 5.20am that I finally managed to get out. Absolutely nothing was going to come of it all – there were no witnesses and nobody was pressing charges. What a waste of time! I could have been catching up on my sleep at home.

But I wasn't going anywhere – at least not at any speed. Rush-hour traffic was building up and I had no chance of getting to Bryan's on time. Still, I'd got cover booked and, pissed off at the waste of a night I'd had, I decided to head straight home, write off the job and get some kip.

But I should have kept a clearer head. Had I done so, I'd have done one last thing – check that the other guy was definitely going to turn up for Bryan.

The message from Bryan's assistant, Ari, was waiting for me when I finally got up, hours later: 'Phone me.' I had an uneasy feeling. Clearly, something had gone very wrong. Immediately, I returned the call.

'What happened?' he demanded. It transpired that the bloke who had promised to cover for me hadn't turned up, so Bryan had been left without a driver.

I explained my side of the story.

'Oh, *man*, he's not going to be happy!'

'Listen – what can I do? It's out of my hands.'

Later, I discovered that the fella working the night shift at the other car firm had failed to transfer the job over to the early-morning crew rota. But that wasn't going to make it any better.

'I guess Bryan will call when he gets back,' said Ari.

And sure enough, we had a conversation. I told him the story and he heard me out.

'Why'd you get involved?'

'At the end of the day,' I said, 'that fella whacked a bird.'

But Bryan was unimpressed. 'I had to run up the street and get a lift with someone,' he told me. Even as he was having a go, I couldn't help smiling to myself on the phone. Typical Bryan Adams! Imagine you're driving along to work when Action Man Adams, one of the world's biggest rock stars, belts up on his tod and flags you down, begging for you to take him to the airport. And the person took him! Well, you would, wouldn't you?

We ended our conversation politely enough. But you know what? He never used me again and I never heard from him again. It was such a shame. We got pretty close – I would say pally. One mistake, that's all it took. And over time, I began to see that maybe I deserved to be given the cold shoulder. The client always has to come first and I'd forgotten that rule. But I could think about it all I liked, I was still gutted at being cut out by him; it was something that definitely hurt. I wouldn't make the same mistake twice. I just wished I hadn't realised it so late.

I really am so sorry, Bryan.

CHAPTER 21

I WILL TAKE A BLADE FOR YOU

It had been a long, hard day and I'd had enough. Leave nothing to chance, though. Just to be on the safe side, I switched the car to the second exit, which wasn't visible from the public side of the restaurant. I was waiting at the door for the client and we walked straight to the car. The engine was running and Ronnie Killick was ready to go. I shut the door and as I tapped the front window to signal all was well, this geezer came from my blind side towards the vehicle. As the car sped off, he raised his hand and I felt what I thought was a hard punch, high up in my side.

Fuck, it really hurt!

I locked his arm up and pulled him to the pavement. Making that movement – *Jesus Christ, it was agony!* Then I saw the claret pouring out of me. How did *that* happen? *Oh, no! Not again*! It wasn't a punch, it was a blade.

Pandemonium.

It wasn't until much later that I had a chance to think about what happened. My client was safely away by the time I was attacked. *Strange*. Was the blade meant for me all along? It was difficult to call. Could just have been a crazy. Possibly. But then I got to thinking that maybe it was a set-up as my mind drifted back to the disagreement I'd had with the artist's assistant.

The artist was a certain Latin-American singer – and I don't want to give out their name – and their assistant had arrived in the UK a couple of days earlier. I'd heard many stories about the assistant's bad behaviour, but it didn't bother me. I was there for the artist and I trusted that if I was going to pick up the assistant first, then at least we might get to know one another and iron out any difficulties before the big name arrived. Some hope.

His attitude was disgusting from the moment he arrived at the airport. He had such a chip. You could see he thought he was more important than his charge. He plonked himself in the back of the motor and took out a DVD from his bag, which he started watching on the in-car system. The peace lasted just a few seconds.

'*These headphones*,' he spat. '*They don't fucking work!*'

He threw them across the car.

'Whoa, whoa, whoa!' I said, holding up a hand. 'What are you doing?'

'I have to make a call,' he said without apology and picked up the car phone.

We had hardly cleared the terminal building and reception was patchy. Anyone who flies regularly should know that. But, no, this twat was off again.

'*This phone – it doesn't fucking work!*'

The handset went flying.

Now I had the hump... he hadn't even been in the car two minutes! I slammed the brakes on.

'Oi! Who the *fuck* d'ya think you are?' I said. 'I suggest you wind your fucking neck in and do as you're told before I sling you out the fucking car, you prick!'

'Oh,' was his only response. I guessed that nobody had ever spoken to him like that. He sat silently with his hands folded neatly on his lap for the entire journey.

Not a word was exchanged once we got to the hotel and I sat in the car while he checked himself in. A woman came out of the hotel, looking rather sheepish.

'Excuse me,' she said, nervously. 'He hasn't finished watching his DVD and wonders if he could have it back, please?'

It was fine by me. I'd said my piece and as far as I was concerned, it was done. I don't bear grudges. The assistant emerged later for a bit of sightseeing. Maybe we could start again? I put on my politest smile.

'Where would you like to go?' I asked.

'Take me to the park,' he said coldly.

Same attitude! He hadn't learned anything.

If you want to start that, I thought, *I'll be the same.*

'*What park?*'

I could keep this up all week if necessary. So did he – all week, until it came to the morning of the artist's arrival. By then I couldn't stand the sight of him. He was such an arrogant prick.

He was all suited for a meeting with a record company that morning. After lunch, he appeared in a tracksuit.

'Are you off to the gym?'

'I'm not going to the fucking gym, man! Take me to the park.'

'*Which park do you want to go to?*'

'Hyde Park.'

'*All right*! I'll take you to Hyde Park.'

'Don't hang around,' he ordered. 'I'll ring.'

Suits me. Much longer and I'd have chinned him. I dropped him at the top end of the park and drove around to Exhibition Road to wait.

The afternoon was getting on and I was beginning to think about going to the airport. The artist was due in around 7pm, but the phone interrupted my thoughts.

'I'm by that golden statue, man.'

He meant the Albert Memorial, just opposite the Albert Hall.

'Pick me up from there.'

At least he was nearby – all I needed to do was a quick u-turn and I was with him.

Hold on – not him, *them*.

Was that him with those three guys? Yes, it was. He was jogging along with his top off, tied around his waist. His friends got in the motor too: one in the front, the other two in the back.

'We need to get something to eat,' said the man sat next to me. He turned to the assistant. 'What are we going to do, darling?'

Darling?

It wasn't long before I became aware of a certain activity in the back. I glanced in the mirror and I didn't like what I saw.

One of the companions was only noshing the assistant off. In the back of my car!

For the second time that week, I slammed on the brakes. It might have been a little uncomfortable for them, but they certainly stopped what they were doing.

'Look, do me a favour here,' I said. 'This is getting a little bit out of hand. I'm not best pleased.'

'It doesn't matter about what pleases *you*,' said the assistant. '*I* employ *you*. Roy, just do as you're told.'

That really peed me off. It wasn't even accurate. I was employed by the artist, not him, the pain in the arse.

We had just got to the top of Bayswater Road by the

park when one of his friends said, 'Why don't we go to a restaurant?'

He leaned forward: 'We'll have enough time, Roy, to go?'

'I think you probably have – I haven't got to be at the airport until the evening.'

I thought it was a perfectly innocent comment, but the assistant had to snap back at me.

'You're not going to the airport,' he told me. 'You're staying with me until *I* say.'

The blanket really had come down now. I hit the brakes – third time.

I always had a back-up car following my lead. Standard procedure. If there was any problem, I needed to be able to transfer the client. Plan B in case anything went wrong. And it had just gone wrong.

'Do yourself a favour and get out of this fucking car now, before I tear your fucking head off, you tosser!'

Three doors flew open. Four bodies scattered. They ran for it, assistant included. I was ready to punch them clean out of the car.

Ronnie screeched to a halt in the back-up vehicle.

What the fuck's going on here?

'What's happened?' shouted Ronnie as he jumped out to help.

'He is a *wanker*!' I said, by way of explanation. Ronnie looked at me as I raged. 'If I see him again, I'm going to punch him all round this fucking place! He's drove me mad all fucking week – he's pushed and pushed and pushed! He can fuck off! I don't want nothing to do with him.'

I was still wound up by the time we had to leave the hotel to pick up the artist. The assistant arrived in the foyer. He hadn't changed his tune.

'You are not going,' he declared.

'Shut up,' I said. 'You ain't telling me nothing! If your boss decides they don't want me, then that's another thing. You have got nothing to do with me, so I suggest you fuck off out of my sight!'

I couldn't give a shit any more. Now I'd lost it, no respect left for the geezer whatsoever.

'We'll see,' he muttered. 'We'll see...'

Ronnie took the assistant in the other car to the airport, where he latched onto his artist as soon as they came through. He got in their car and one of my other staff and Ronnie and I had to follow in the second vehicle. I didn't really care. I knew that he would be in the singer's ear all the way back to London to try and get rid of me. Big mistake! The artist had done their homework and knew they had the best. I guessed the artist also realised how difficult the assistant could be.

He got out of the car at the hotel and the assistant had a smug, 'you're fired' air about him.

The artist had a quiet word: 'I'm in a bit of a predicament here.'

'Yeah, I know,' I replied. 'At the end of the day, if you want me to step down, I'll step down. It's not a problem...'

'No, no, no,' was the response. 'I don't want that! But you'll have to keep away from him.'

And for the rest of the visit, the assistant and I were kept away from one another.

The artist was known for sleeping in late and spending ages getting ready before heading out for the evening. Their nights out were grand performances and the artist wouldn't step out of the hotel until they looked absolutely amazing – and they had a massive entourage to help them. That, and a Luton van-load of luggage for the few days they were over, which would ensure they had an outfit for every conceivable occasion.

We headed for a top London restaurant that I'd been to countless times before. I knew how to get my clients in there better than I knew how to get in my own house. It should have been routine. The journey passed without incident and we waited outside the venue until about ten minutes before they were ready to leave. Everything was quiet. Clockwork. Then the call came through that we had to bring the cars up. And as I got the artist away, that's when that bloke came at me with the knife.

Why does it always happen to me? But I knew the answer: it comes with the job. At some point, the bodyguard will be in the line of fire. You might go ten years without anything happening, and if you do, well done. Count your lucky stars! But some day it may happen. And you never know how you will react until it does. You might *think* you know, but I can assure you that you don't.

I had to get the wound sorted out at the hospital. *Here we go again*. It had almost become routine. The nurse took me into the cubicle and cauterised the wound – a familiar sensation – patched me up and left me to recover.

Back at the hotel the next day, the pain having worn off a bit, it was almost time to do the airport transfer. I reassured the artist that there was nothing they could have done. I knew what to say; I'd been in this sort of situation before. Too many times, you might think. I noticed that the assistant tended to look away whenever I spoke. He wasn't really engaged in the conversation, it was as if he wasn't interested. I wondered again about the convenience of a random attack by an opportunist. There was something about the assistant's studied air of casual indifference which set alarm bells ringing.

But I would never know – and what was the good of brooding? Nobody had been killed and the artist was more than happy with the way I did the job. The last few hours of their stay went smoothly. Ronnie and I left the airport together and made for the car.

'Ron...' I started.

'Don't even say it.'

'Say *what*? You don't know what I'm about to come out with.'

'Yeah. Yeah, I do. You need some time for yourself.'

And I did. He was right. I needed a break.

I took a month off. It had got to the point where I didn't even know if I wanted to continue with the job at all. I confessed my inner turmoil to Mr J – he had the stake in the company, after all.

'I'm not surprised,' he said. 'What do you want to do? I need to know.'

At that point, it was just the holiday, but underneath it all I was thinking, *I've had enough of this game*. And, as ever, it was my darling Joanne who expressed it best.

'How many times are you going to put yourself in danger for these people?' she asked. 'You've got to start thinking of us now.'

It was good advice. And I listened to it for... oh, at least a couple of days. After a week of doing nothing, I was over the shock and ready to get back to work. After about three weeks at home, I have to admit, I was climbing the fucking walls! Then it came to me.

You know what? I thought to myself. *I'd like to train – I could be an instructor.* That would give me more balance in my life. And it would provide a great opportunity to pass on my innovations and style of doing the job.

'What a good idea!' said Ronnie and he pointed out

that the company offices had a massive yard. We had everything down there that we could possibly need.

I would be chief instructor. Some of the longer-serving boys could teach alongside me. They hadn't been in the game as long as me, but I was thinking of colleagues Steve Marshall, Kritch and Ronnie. They had a lot to give. I thought that Mr J would be up for coming in with us as we expanded, but I was soon to discover that he had plans of his own.

Ronnie phoned while I was still on my sabbatical to report that Mr J was taking an interest in one of the actresses from *EastEnders*. He had never trained as a bodyguard, but he still thought he could step into my shoes while I was absent. At the time I guessed he liked the thrill and the glamour of the work. I soon discovered that wasn't all he was enjoying.

'You'll never guess where I am,' said Ronnie. 'In the West End with Mr J.'

'What are you doing there?' I asked.

'He's out with that actress from *EastEnders*.'

'*Whaddya mean he's out*?'

Ronnie knew what my reaction would be: I won't allow socialising with clients. That's why he knew that he had to tell me about it.

'He's having dinner.'

'What the *fuck* are you talking about?'

But I knew, and Ronnie knew. It's the one thing you don't do, the one thing guaranteed to pee me off: overstepping the line, getting familiar with a client. But Mr J never mentioned that evening to me and after I returned to work, it all went quiet for a bit.

Then after New Year, he came out with it: it had got to the point where he couldn't *not* tell me.

'Oh, by the way, I have to let you know: I'm seeing that *EastEnders* girl.'

Then I twigged. This was what it had all been about for Mr J. All it had ever been about. Investing the money, getting the work, setting up the firm, getting the clients, establishing a name… All he ever wanted was to be a celebrity himself. At least that's how it seemed to me. And if he couldn't do it himself, maybe he felt he could be someone by attaching himself to a celebrity and becoming famous by proxy. I felt that I'd been totally let down.

'How can we continue working together?' I asked.

'Well, I know,' he replied. 'It might be best if you have the security firm and I step away from it completely. It's all yours.'

'Well, I know it's mine,' I said. 'It's me, anyway!'

I hadn't expected his next move, but that same week he emptied the bank account. That went down a treat, with a payroll going out. It was a sour end. And Mr J and I had got on like a house on fire at first. We had a good understanding, but it just couldn't be the same once he'd started carrying on the way he did.

He and the girl from *EastEnders* went on to get married and they've got a kid as well. I heard they'd sold the story of their wedding to a magazine. Annoyingly, the press still reported that he was the boss of the security firm. Clients would read about his life in the tabloids and wonder if his old firm could still be trusted to be discreet. They didn't realise he had nothing to do with us now. The phones went quiet as a result. I'd done jack shit, he'd crossed over the line, but I was the one getting punished. The *EastEnders* PAs dried up. I don't think Mr J ever realised what damage he'd done. We went into a real crisis for a while.

PPP should have gone down there and then, but as time

went on and everyone calmed down a bit, clients began to think straight and realised that the security had always been about Roy. Mr J was money. I was pretty lucky though, but somehow we got through it.

Meanwhile, I continued with the plan to open my own training college. I found my own premises and funded the college personally; I was determined to make it work.

We taught three courses – basic, intermediate and full advanced. Everyone had to do the basic before they went on, no matter how much experience they already had. It was taught over a weekend, 9am–6pm. Saturday was a sort of introduction, but on Sunday trainees were graded and any mistakes counted against the final mark. I placed the pass rate at 75 per cent. And you had to get even more, 80 per cent, to be considered for the intermediate course. By the time you reached the advanced, you had to be looking to achieve more than 95 per cent to get through.

I was insistent my students didn't think that for me, this was purely a moneymaking venture. I knew the time and cash would be a significant investment for a lot of hopefuls and so, if someone passed but not by enough to allow them to start the next level, I let them redo the weekend without charge. And I said that if, after that they still felt they hadn't learned enough, then I would refund the full cost of the course. I couldn't say fairer than that.

Recruits came from all walks of life, though the majority of applications were from doormen. And a lot of them seemed to think bodyguarding was something out of *James Bond*. Or they'd try to act all mean and moody, and I'd have to remind them to smile. Put people at their ease. You're supposed to look after the client, not terrify the poor bastard.

Our basic course covered D-bus, E-bus, Long Reach and

Short Reach – in other words, entering and exiting a building, positioning a vehicle and getting to it. As the trainees practised formations, I'd play the VIP.

The intermediate course was a lot longer and the advanced took place abroad because it involved firearms training. We would relocate to Eastern European countries, where we could use the military firing ranges. But it was very rare that any of the students got that far. Those who did, I usually advised to go with one of the main schools like Phoenix – the big training school out in the USA, who recognised my basic and intermediate certificates. Phoenix's facilities are amazing – I'm talking a multi-million dollar establishment. The camp includes a whole mock town complete with shops and actors playing inhabitants. They have state-of-the-art vehicles and do kidnap-and-retrieve exercises, in which they play out scenarios like a car being rammed – and they actually do this for real. But that was way down the line for all those I was training. Most would never make it that far.

However, it was always nice to hear from the graduates who did well, especially in my later years. Peter George Piper was one of those. My finest protégé, he just went straight through the ranks. He was an exceptional bodyguard and he went on to work with the likes of Janet Jackson. I'm so proud of him, I really am proud. He's a lovely lad. I think he's in his 40s now – catching up with me, bless him. And he's the only guy who's always stayed in touch. He'll often ring for advice and to let me know how things are going. All his clients ask him to stay with them permanently and I always advise him not to hang about so long that you get soft and complacent.

So he tells them, 'You know what? I learned from the best – and Roy Snell *is* the best!' It does make me laugh;

it's amazing how many say that. I was once asked to do a magazine interview when a film featuring bodyguards came out and some 86 per cent of people surveyed in the industry said the same thing – 'Roy Snell, he's Britain's ultimate bodyguard'. And so that was the headline they used.

*****

Peter George Piper: 'Wednesday 11 October is a day I will never forget. I'll start with what I live by – like attracts like and the cream always rises to the top. You write your own history.

'I had to go to the dentist to have my tooth taken out on the 13th. Right painful. I remember very clearly the dentist saying, "Hot salt water will stop the bleeding," and it did – after rolling around my front room like a man who had just got severely hit in the mouth.

'I also remember the day because Reg Kray was being buried and I wanted to go to the funeral, but I couldn't. Ladies and gentlemen, boys and girls – sounds like a pantomime but it's not. Remember, people come into your life for a reason or a season or a lifetime.

'Monday, 16 October I'm starting my new job at a car firm based in north-west London. I'll never forget it. I walked into the office and I was told sit down by Martin. There were four people in that room – there was a bodyguard standing against the window to the left, a secretary who had a bird's-eye view of me, and the owner sitting to the right. Meanwhile, there was another office to the right, but the door was closed.

'Three minutes later I can hear the blokes in that office talking. One voice is getting louder. The bodyguard to the left of me is repeatedly flicking his fag in the ashtray. Then he drops the line from hell: "Any minute now, he's gonna throw him through that partition." I wondered if he was trying to give me a moral boost?

'Luckily enough, the argument ended. All of a sudden the door opens and Roy Snell walks out. I will never forget the way he looked at me. He looks at his mate Ronnie and said, "He's one. I can see it in his eyes." The acceptance, the friendship, whatever you want to call it, was instant. Straightaway my security course started.

'Within a week, Roy got the contract for the Russian Chess Championship. That was some experience for me! At the weekend I was doing my basic training with Roy. My nickname for him is "the Colonel" – he is sharp as a blade and brilliant at raising your spirits. He could have been a comedian; he would have pissed it. These days, I just tell him to turn it down, but he never listens. Once he gets on a roll he knows he's got me and I'm the world's worst: I cry like a river with laughter.

'I worked for the car firm for all of five months, but had to move on in the end. Roy and Ronnie did exactly the same; it's a shame. We were looking after people who really appreciated what we did.

'Then I worked for a firm covering the music business and I was sat in my front room one day, just cracked open a Guinness and the mobile went. "Nursery," they called me. "Just been on the phone to your guv'nor..." The name "Nursery Rhyme" has stuck ever since. How could it not? Classic! Thank you, Mr Snell... Piper out...'

CHAPTER 22

MEET THE LOAF

It was when we got to the airport that I realised we had a problem. The transfer was routine, everything was in place, but...

'What do we call him, Ron? *Meat?* Or Mr Loaf?'

Through the VIP exit appeared the man himself: larger than life, but travelling light; just one companion. I introduced myself.

'Hi Roy,' he rasped. 'How ya doing?'

'Well, me and my colleague here have been discussing something... The thing is... what do we call ya?'

He gave a belly laugh and then roared 'You kin call me... *Meat*!' I warmed to him – another big guy with a big personality. It was a bit like meeting a long-lost brother.

'Oh, all right!' I said, 'Okay, mate!'

Meat Loaf had done his autobiography about the same time that we'd got the contract to cover publicity tours for Virgin Books. We did everyone from Peter Schmeichel to the lovely Meat. One of the first was David Ginola, though I'm not that up on football and so I didn't know that much about him: big name in the game, apparently. Meat was to do a talk at Oxford University. The President of the Union was so impressed by the way we handled the night that he asked us to do other events for them and when he heard Meat Loaf was in town, he called to ask if he would come down to address the students.

Meat Loaf had a packed itinerary and the first stop was Birmingham, but I wondered if he'd want to rest in a hotel first. We had time, and we'd got him a room in his favourite hotel, the Landmark.

'No, let's go straight to Birmingham, buddy.' Meat had this incredible energy and this exuberant public persona, but I would spend a lot of time with him over the next few days and I noticed that in private he often seemed drained. When he wasn't 'on', when he wasn't being Meat, he just seemed to sink into himself. He revealed that he suffered badly from insomnia.

'Some nights I get an hour – sometimes just 45 minutes,' he told me. 'If I get more than that, I call it a good night.' He really wasn't a well man. Bless him! You'd never know it to see him in action. And by the time we got to Birmingham, we were laughing our heads off like old mates – he was just such an easy person to get on with despite the exhaustion he must feel all day; it was unreal. I put my men under strict instructions to leave him be if he happened to fall asleep while we were driving him. It might be the best kip he'd had in weeks.

As we got back to the hotel in London that night, he stopped me.

'Buddy, can I ask you a favour?'

I turned to him. He'd got suddenly serious.

'Yeah, of course you can.'

'I don't need all this,' he said, gesturing towards the other security guys and including the two vehicles we had in his sweep. 'I don't like it. You and Ron, that's all I need.'

Though I appreciated how relaxed Meat felt with us, I also needed to consider his safety. I wasn't so much concerned about having a big entourage for chat shows and the like – what I called 'babysitting' jobs – but I wouldn't take him on my own to clubs, parties or anywhere there might be lots of fans. How many times did I drum it into my own recruits? The three most important numbers in bodyguarding are three, six and zero – for 360 degrees. You need to be able to see all round your client when you can't guarantee the situation. I'd rather have them use another firm than be forced to look after them on my jack, no matter who they are or how cool they feel about things. Yet I figured that between us, Ronnie and I were enough to cover the 360 for Meat. But it's surprising how much greater concern there has been about keeping the costs down since I left the game. These days, I see far more stars with just one bodyguard – I wouldn't have allowed it.

So the next day, it was just Ronnie and me who turned up for Meat. I gave him the news about the Oxford Union talk. He was over the moon, seriously made up; it was such an honour for him to be asked. And he's hardly inexperienced in pulling a crowd. He puts everything into a show, gives it absolutely everything. This is a man who barely sleeps and yet he practically crawls off the stage when he's finished performing! It's where he lives, bless him. But even for him, the prospect of going to Oxford, with all its hundreds of years of history, was something special, the kind of crowd he'd never played before.

The students gave him a rapturous welcome. They leapt to their feet, cheering and applauding, before he even said a word. It was an easy gig for me and Ronnie. We just stood at the back of the hall and enjoyed Meat's speech. Afterwards, he stayed on at the lectern and took questions from the audience while the student President sat next to him.

'Is true that you're starting to lose your vocal power?' asked one cheeky little sod.

'Rumours... Chinese whispers... they can hurt your career,' began Meat softly. 'They can crucify you...' He paused dramatically, gripped the lecture stand, and without warning belted out, '*LIKE A BAT OUTTA HELL...*' Grown men covered their ears as the windows rattled. And that was Meat without the mic. I swear, the foundations shook. I tried to imagine what it would sound like with proper amplification. *Bloody hell!* I thought, *Meat! Jesus, mate!*

There was a stunned silence. Meat looked thoughtfully out at the crowd for a moment, then he switched his gaze to the smart-arse student who asked the question.

'Whaddya reckon, honey?' he asked sweetly. 'Do *you* think I've lost it?'

Everyone cheered and laughed. They adored him and his own obvious enjoyment was infectious.

There was a reception for him upstairs, but it was very studenty, not what I'd call an aftershow party – a few sandwiches and stuff. Looked more like afternoon tea to me. But you know what students are like – give them half a bleedin' shandy and six straws, and they're all pissed!

Then came Meat's finest moment. It hadn't been the evening's speech, the questions or the laughter... it was when they asked him to sign the book.

Each speaker at the Oxford Union leaves their signature in this formal document. Meat obligingly leaned over the table and added his. 'You know... this is a great honour...'

he began formally. Then he looked at the rest of that page and saw the name two above his. '*Holy shit*! Hey, Roy! C'm here!' he yelled. '*Man!* Can you believe that shit?' I peered over his shoulder to see that former US President Bill Clinton had recently been in town. And with childlike delight and enthusiasm, Meat pointed towards his own addition: 'And there's *me*!'

The book tour took up most of the remainder of Meat's stay and that's when the security had to get more serious.

'Look, Meat, tomorrow mate, you've got a massive signing in the Glades, in Bromley,' I explained. 'Sorry, it ain't just gonna be two. It can't! I gotta have at least six, maybe eight guys. I've got to have an outer ring and an inner ring. Just me and Ronnie by you, but we'll have those other guys spread out as well, just keeping an eye out.'

But Meat understood what we needed to do and told me I could just get on with it, 'buddy'. Everything was 'buddy' with him.

He was due to make his appearance at 2pm. On the day, Ronnie called the venue at regular intervals to check how many fans were waiting. We didn't want to turn up mob-handed to find the place empty and us embarrassed. You want to know if you have to take the client out and round the block a couple of times to drum up an audience – though with someone as phenomenally popular as Meat this was unlikely to happen.

Ron looked up from the phone after his 1pm check-in. I didn't even need to ask when I saw his face.

'How many?' I grinned.

There was a soft sigh from Ronnie's side of the room.

'*Go on!*'

'They reckon about 1,500 at the moment, but that's just a guess – the queue's going round the block.'

'You're *kidding* me!' I said. 'We told 'em to cap it at a thousand.'

And there was still an hour or so to go.

'Yeah, apparently they're just queuing anyway. And they ain't budging, mate.'

We smuggled Meat through the back entrance of the shopping centre, down a ramp into the staff car park, where the Glades top brass had turned out in force, along with a contingent from the bookshop. You'd think they were there to welcome a visiting head of state. It did make me chuckle. They were all so over-excited. I always think it's strange the way people react to celebrity. Meat loved it – he just loves the fact that people adore him.

Up in the shop I scanned the surroundings. The store was topped with a dome and was on two levels, like an old-fashioned library, with a gallery running around above us. The staff pointed out where Meat would be sitting. It wasn't hard to spot – it was the desk that sprouted a queue snaking all the way out the door, into the centre itself and into the distance.

'Meat, you seeing this?'

'Yeah, buddy, I know, man,' he said. 'But you know what? I'm gonna stay here until *you* tell me that queue is ended or until you decide to stop it. And I'm gonna stay here until I've signed everyone.'

That's the sort of guy he was – he wasn't frightened of hard graft.

I decided the only way to get a decent number of folk through was to limit what Meat wrote. There would be no personalised messages, just his signature. And then he would stay back to do a few copies for the employees of the shop itself.

Ronnie and I walked the length of the queue with Kritch.

There must have been 2,500 people at least. I estimated how many we'd realistically have time to do, then I added on a couple of hundred, just to be generous. But it had to end somewhere and inevitably there were going to be some disappointed fans.

'Kritch, stop it here. Stay here,' I said. 'There's no more after that. They ain't gonna get done, mate.'

There were some people who wouldn't take no for an answer and were determined to wait. But it was up to them – it wasn't going to happen. Personally, I doubted even Meat would have the stamina to sit there long enough to do what we had, let alone more.

Finally, we were off.

Meat kept up a light-hearted banter and his fans were very friendly. He even did a couple of photos. *Yes,* I thought, *lovely. But don't keep doing that, mate – it's going to take a lot longer!*

I kept myself on my toes. Always looking, scanning up... scanning down. Doing 'the clock' – 9, 12, 3 and occasionally 10, 1, 2. (Don't worry about 6pm – that's the floor.)

Ronnie was behind me, completing the 360-degree view, doing the other side.

And then I saw him.

Geezer on the upper level: full-length leather coat.

There was something about him. I don't know what, you just go on your instincts a lot of the time. Body language? The way he was looking? Something. But I had to listen to those internal alarm bells. If I was wrong, I could always apologise. And if I happened to be right and didn't act on it, the consequences could be devastating.

What is this muppet doing?

I looked around at my staff. A deliberate glance at Kevin,

at Neil. *Are you seeing this, fellas*? I looked up at the suspect fella. I repeated the looks, nothing abrupt or panicky. You might miss it if you didn't know what we were doing, but it was all they needed. Even without me speaking, my men knew when their guv'nor had given an order.

The pair headed upstairs, also moving purposefully but not so quickly they might provoke a reaction before they were close enough to deal with it. I continued to watch. Ronnie copped what was going on and positioned himself on the far side of Meat's desk.

The geezer in the coat was still looking over the balcony, completely unaware that Neil and Kevin were standing at the back of the upper level behind him, one on either side.

Without any warning, the fella's left hand reached for his inside pocket. My heart fluttered.

Everything went very quickly after then.

As that left hand pulled out, I could see a glimpse of something – I couldn't see what and there wasn't the time to find out.

Shit!

I dived onto the desk and slid along.

Ronnie appeared behind Meat, yanking him backwards and to the side. It wasn't gentle, but he would be safe.

I glided inelegantly into the line of fire, across the desk and ended up on the floor in a heap. Silence.

And then I heard a sound from Meat Loaf.

Laughter.

I'm glad you find it funny because I've really fucking hurt my elbow!

I picked myself up and looked down – what was on the floor? *A fucking sausage!* The geezer thought it would be a laugh to throw meat at Meat. My boys had already grabbed him and spun him round.

Downstairs, a couple of fans were standing by the desk: two girls who followed Meat everywhere. They were at the telly studios, the Oxford Union and at every signing. I think Meat phoned them himself to let them know where he was!

'I bet you feel stupid,' they said smugly.

'Not really,' I said. 'At least I've done my job.'

And Meat continued to do his.

I think he must have spent more than four hours signing those books in the shop. Even I was amazed by his stamina. We walked him back down to the car and I felt elated. It had been a really good day, though I knew the trivial interruption could easily have turned out to be something quite serious – you never knew.

Meat spent the rest of the signing bantering with us: 'Stand in front of me, boys! It might be a leg of lamb next! Or some spare ribs!'

But when we were almost at the car, he put his hand on my shoulder and looked very seriously at me. I'll never forget what he said next.

'Now I know, buddy,' he said, quietly. 'I just wanted to let you know – *I know*.' And his eyes said it all. Despite all the piss-taking, he understood that I'd put my life on the line for him.

As we arrived at the airport on his last day, he presented me with a signed copy of his book.

'I don't want you to read it until I go,' he warned.

After he left, I sat in the car and laughed out loud when I saw what he'd added.

'To Roy,' he had written. 'Please send me all of your operatives as soon as possible. Need help. Being attacked by young, beautiful women. Help!' Only Meat!

We'd really established a great rapport and became, in a way, good buddies over the rest of his stay.

Friendships go like that in bodyguarding. They can be very intense – while they last; it's in the nature of the work that you're very close to someone for a period of time. It might be anything from a day to a few months, but you're closer to them than anyone else – you have to be prepared to do anything for them. But they can just as easily forget you, very easily.

But sometimes it works in exactly the opposite way.

I was in a club off-duty when a huge Hollywood star turned up. The manager came up to the friend I was with and told him who was about to arrive.

'That's all right,' my mate said, 'Roy's here.'

Hold on a minute! I'm not grafting here! I've just come down as a guest.

'Would you mind walking him down and walking him in?'

'Well, I'd have liked to have enjoyed my night off,' I said to my mate. 'Thanks for putting me in the line for it. That makes you look ten times better, doesn't it?'

The manager was very grateful.

'May I ask who the client is?'

'It's Will Smith.'

Turning up unannounced to a nightclub? No wonder they were a bit desperate! But I have to say, when I met him outside to tell him that I was going to take him to the VIP section, he was a lovely fella. He was probably the biggest star on the planet, but he was very down-to-earth.

'Roy, can I have one of your cards?' he asked, as he went to leave. I assumed he was just being polite and maybe he read that in my face, because he said, 'No, I'm serious. I'm taking this for a reason. I like your style, man. You're very relaxed, you're very calm. I like it.'

I was impressed by the way he made the effort to be

respectful and when we left, he pointed me out to the bodyguards he'd brought from America.

'Hey, guys, I don't want any heavy-handed stuff here. Remember who you're with. Roy – would you mind taking the lead?'

That was the way it went in my game. You never knew when your reputation would suddenly make you a new friend and get you an 'in' when you weren't even working. But it certainly wasn't a regular 9-to-5 job. You couldn't always tell when you were going to clock off.

Like the day of the Spice Girls' last-ever gig in December 2000, when I organised transportation and had to make sure that the club was all sorted out for the aftershow party.

We inspected the West End venue's entrances and exits, and I went through where I would walk down the girls.

'Were the local authorities okay about barriers and so on?' I asked the owner. But he looked blank. Not a good sign, not promising at all.

The Spice Girls were only the biggest band on the entire planet. This was only their final appearance together. It might be reasonable to assume the public would be showing a bit of interest in the passing of the legendary girl band.

'Which local authorities?' he asked, not entirely reassuringly. *This,* I thought, *is getting better by the minute.* One of my pet hates is working with amateurs. What would have happened if I wasn't experienced enough to ask? Nothing, that's what. And that could mean big trouble, especially on a night as big as this.

You couldn't rely on the location of the aftershow party being a secret. The fans always find out. And if every bloody Spice Girl fan in the country turned up outside this club, someone would get seriously hurt. Streets close down very quickly. Havoc.

I got on the phone and West End Central police were not best pleased to be told so late in the day about the treat in store. Usually, they provided a van with officers who waited at one end of the street out of the way in case it got out of hand. That wasn't a problem; it was standard, but it needed to be done in time. Time was running out.

'We need to get barriers out there as well,' I told the owner. I had no idea if he was aware of how big a favour I was doing him by letting him know what he needed to do. Maybe he thought I was sticking my oar in, but if all hell broke loose and it was down to him not telling the police about his special guests, his club was in for a massive fine.

By the time the Spice Girls pulled up in their limos, already something like a thousand screaming fans thronged the street and they yelled all the louder as I walked each member of the group into the club.

The party went really well; everyone had a whale of a time. My old and dear friend Frank was there – he was Mel C's personal CPO (Close Protection Officer) and he did everything for her. I hadn't seen him for ages.

'*Christ!* Good to see you, Earholes!' Frank's got enormous lugs and I'm one of the few people who've known him long enough to get away with calling him that.

We chatted for a while and then Frank pointed out another bodyguard. It wasn't someone I knew, but apparently he was looking after one of the other Spice Girls and her husband. Frank hadn't heard of this bodyguard either, but the fella was making himself out to be a bit of a hero. The Spice Girl's family had been receiving really nasty threats in the post and he'd been putting it about that he was the only one who could deal with it.

'Something about the guy doesn't ring true,' Frank told me.

'Well, I can ask a friend of mine,' I said. Chucky – he'd know if there was anything dodgy about this fella. 'No problem. Leave it with me.'

There didn't seem to be any immediate hurry, so I got through the rest of the party and called Chucky the next day. He agreed to look into it for me and called back a few days later.

'No, mate,' he said, 'No one knows him.'

That set alarm bells ringing. The elite bodyguard world isn't that big: everyone knows everyone else and you keep coming across the same faces at different events. Where had this geezer come from? I let Frank know what Chucky said.

We weren't the only ones to voice suspicions among the family staff and it soon turned out this geezer had organised the intimidation himself in an effort to make himself look good. He figured that if they were scared, then they would be more likely to use him. He didn't count on everyone else watching out for them. Very soon, he was out of a job.

I'm not sure if he was ever charged or convicted of anything in court, but it wasn't my concern once he was away from the circuit. As soon as his little game was discovered, he was blacklisted. He'd never work as a bodyguard again.

The Spice Girls remained massively popular, even after that last night, and I next came across one of them, Mel C, at the Party in the Park. Often the artists playing those big Hyde Park gigs book rooms in one of the major hotels over the road to use as glorified dressing rooms. They only need to nip over the road and they're in the venue. It's much more comfortable than anything you could have backstage at the gig itself.

We'd been allocated All Saints and we were at the Metropole Hotel at the start of what was usually quite a long day. On those days you'd be forever ferrying them over and back for rehearsals, soundchecks and what have you. This mini-festival was particularly draining and then the artists went back to their hotels for a bit of a party that went on right through the night – and I mean all the way through the night. At 7.30am Shaznay finally came out of the hotel and I got ready to take her home. Fortunately, she only lived up the road – thank God – in W2. Mel was being taken by my colleague Frankie. She was a local girl as well, but she came out with a mate who lived somewhere in the middle of Hertfordshire. Poor old Frankie had to take her all the way!

Just as I was congratulating myself on picking the easy job, Shaznay piped up, 'Oh hang on, can you take one of my friends? They're just coming down.'

You're having a Tufnell, ain't you? I'm knackered!

She disappeared upstairs again and nothing happened. It continued not to happen until about 9am, by which time I'd had quite enough and buzzed up to their room.

'Look, if no one's coming down,' I said, pretty fed up by then. '*I-am-going-home*. I'm not sitting here anymore. You've had your night, you're back indoors – and that's it for me!'

By then, I was getting to the point of being dangerously tired. If it went on much longer, I'd be in no fit state to drive anywhere.

Minutes later, Mel C appeared.

'Why have you come downstairs?' I asked grumpily.

'I'm the peace offering.'

'I just want to go home.'

She gave me a kiss on the cheek, saying, 'Thanks, darling, for everything you've done.'

It was sweet of her to say sorry, but that night was a reminder for me that the bodyguard job isn't done until the artist is home and in bed – even if you're not.

CHAPTER 23

BACK FOR GOOD

Take That's reunion felt like unfinished business for me, too. We'd got on so well together first time around – I was there at the very end of the first half of their career, one of the last concerts at Wembley Arena in 1996. I'd walked them onto the stage then, and now I couldn't wait to see them again.

As I drove to the Marriott in London, where Mark and Jason were staying while the band recorded ITV's *An Audience with Take That*, I had a big grin on my face. I was early, which gave me an opportunity to have some fun.

I parked the motor just past the entrance so I had my back to the doors and they couldn't see my face. Then I watched for them in the mirror. *There was Mark!* Out first, having a fag while gossiping on his mobile. Before he had a chance to reach for the door, I turned round.

'Yeah, yeah, darling...' he stopped abruptly.

'*Roy... Roy? Roy!*'

He was still holding the phone as he bellowed in shock. His missus on the other end must have thought he'd gone completely mad. I got out of the car and he virtually leapt into my arms, a kid all over again.

'If you think I'm gonna wipe your arses this time around,' I laughed, 'you've got another thing coming!'

'Have you seen Jason?' he asked.

'No, no...'

'Well, get in the car then, before he knows it's you!'

Sure enough, Jason was too busy chatting with Mark to clock who was up front. Mark interrupted him.

'You should say hello to the driver...'

I glanced in the mirror and turned round.

'*Holy shit, Roysie!*' shouted Jason.

'Yes,' I said solemnly. 'I'm back, gentlemen. Good job you've got someone who knows what they're doing, eh?'

It was only a short journey, but we had such a laugh. They wouldn't let anyone else take them for the rest of the tour.

Record companies own big houses in town that they keep for their artists – I had to pick up Gary Barlow from one in Kensington. As he came out of the grand gates of the company pad, he seemed preoccupied.

'So you're not going to say hello, then?' I asked, as he got in.

Gary's reaction was much the same as I'd got off the other boys. The old times came flooding back for him, too.

'Yeah,' I said, 'Bin a while innit? And what about you, then? You don't phone... don't write...' We reached Abbey Road Studios and I got a big hug from him.

'Roy, it's just so nice,' said Gary. 'Do you know what? I forgot about your sense of humour.'

They all knew there were no airs and graces with me. And I think that's the way the record company saw it – that I knew the boys and that put them at their ease, helped them relax.

Looking back now, I find it amazing to think that Take That were just one of so many acts I was working with that I can barely remember all their names. I didn't realise it then, but I was putting my health at great risk with the amount I was taking on and yet I really enjoyed my work. It seemed that no sooner had I finished with one band, another would appear. Often they were completely different types of performer but but some would always stand out.

One thing about BB King was that he always travelled with the rest of his band. And in the UK, that meant a six-seater Chrysler Voyager. At the airport, he was unmistakable – a massive guy, even now he was quite old, and like all his band, immaculately dressed. Then there was Spats – yes, wearing a pair of spats with his suit – who must have been in his 80s. He introduced himself by explaining his nickname was for what he did with his spats: there and then, he started tap-dancing. Like the Pied Piper I led the way, with old Spats tapping energetically the whole way to the bloody motor!

'I'm gonna ask you to do me a favour,' BB King began, as we set off.

Oh, shit, I thought. *Here we go!*

'I'm gonna give you some money and I need you to do something for me...'

I knew it. Drugs. Girls. All the way to the Royal Garden Hotel in Kensington my mind raced while I tried to keep up a cheerful conversation. I was thinking about how I would turn him down without sounding disrespectful. What the hell was he going to ask for? It was doing my head in.

We pulled up outside, the luggage following in another vehicle. The hotel made the biggest fuss of BB King you can imagine. He always gets the biggest suite – he gets completely spoilt when he's there. He hasn't got to leave the room for anything, if he doesn't want to.

BB pulled out a wad of dollars. 'I want my usual...' he drawled. 'Six portions of fish'n'chips and mushy peas.'

I almost burst out laughing with relief: one portion for everyone in the band, now that's rock'n'roll...

I can tell you I was in a far more relaxed frame of mind driving the short distance to the restaurant. It was a real family place – father and son were behind the counter. I smiled at the younger man, but no sooner had I given the order than his dad looked up sharply.

'Is *he* in town?' he asked, with something approaching reverence in his voice.

'Sorry?' I said. But even as I did so, my eyes went to the wall behind him, where a picture of BB King in action took pride of place. He clocked my glance.

'Please send him my regards,' he said. It was left to his son to explain the story as the old man's attention was taken by the next customer.

'You'll have to excuse Dad,' said the lad, as he dished up the order. 'He's got to be one of BB King's biggest fans. He's followed him for *years*. We found out from the last guy like yourself where the food was going. That picture up there? Dad's favourite possession.'

As I drove back, an idea was starting to form in my mind. Maybe? Maybe not. Let's see how things go. I delivered the food to the hotel kitchen to be reheated and sent up to the band's suite.

The gig was at the Apollo in Hammersmith and the next day, I took the boys down for their soundcheck. It was the usual routine for me – checking backstage, and clearing and securing the entrances; I'd done it a thousand times. But then

I got a chance to chat to Spats when he was away from the rest of the band and, more importantly, BB King. I didn't want it to seem as if I were stepping out of line but I thought maybe the man himself should know that his number one fan was also his favourite chef in London. I didn't say that I knew it would make his year, let alone his day, to get a signed picture for his collection. Immediately Spats understood.

'Really?' he said thoughtfully. 'Leave it with me, I'll see what I can do.'

At their advanced age, the band couldn't play more than alternate nights but when they did take to the stage, they were phenomenal. The venue was packed to the rafters. Great show.

Afterwards, I went to check if I was needed on their day off. Spats beckoned me over.

'How far is it from the hotel to this little restaurant?'

I explained it wasn't far. Depending on traffic it could be as quick as 20 minutes.

'Meet us at half past one,' he said, a mischievous twinkle in his eye. 'He's gonna *go* to that fish shop.'

He laughed when he saw my face. Maybe a photo or something... but I hadn't been expecting a personal appearance.

And, to be honest, from my professional point of view while it might have been a nice gesture it was a bloody nightmare – taking a blues legend to a West London chippie! Me and my big mouth…

As we drove over that lunchtime I began to get nervous about the public reaction. What if he got mobbed?

'Excuse me,' I said, 'Would you mind losing the hat? Just the hat.'

It wasn't half distinctive. I thought that people would at least have to look twice maybe to recognise him. He saw the point and I played it safe by leaving the car out of the way around the corner and telling Ronnie to guard it.

'Let's try to play this down,' I said. 'I just wanna walk in and get this over *very* quickly.'

Ronnie nodded his agreement.

It was after the main lunch rush and there were only two or three people in front of us as I walked in. The owner looked up and his eyes widened when I stepped to one side and BB King and Spats arrived.

'I hear you're the one we gotta thank for our fish and chips and mushy peas,' said BB King. The owner stared silently, tears rolling down his face. He couldn't believe it... he blubbed away silently.

I do love it when clients do things like this.

BB smiled warmly at the owner: 'Looks like you might need a hand!' he declared, lifting up the counter hatch and marching through to the other side.

He only picked up a bleedin' chef's hat and put it on!

'Can I help you, ma'am?' enquired the world's greatest blues guitarist of the next customer. 'You want some of these here fish'n'chips? I kin recommend them personally!'

The owner's son had already dived under the counter, raced out and disappeared through the adjoining entrance to the flat above the shop. Seconds later, he reappeared, gasping for breath and clutching a camera.

'Would... would you mind, Roy?' he asked.

'I'm sure he would be fine,' I said. 'A photo all right, Spats?'

'Hey, Roy!' said Spats. 'We're with friends here, man!'

So the newest employee was pictured spooning out the grub while the shop's owner stood, still open-mouthed, beside him.

I drove the two musicians directly to the soundcheck from the chippie.

'You know, I've worked with some artists from all

around the world,' I said, 'and I have to say that's probably one of the nicest things I've ever known someone to do.'

BB King paused and then he spoke quietly, but his words hit me like a sledgehammer to the guts.

'I remember what it was like when I worked in the Cotton Club,' he said. 'I worked and worked and worked for a dollar, two dollars a week. I know how hard things can be. I haven't always been this successful and I never take it for granted. It's people like that, like those two in that restaurant, who put me where I am today. I'll never forget that.'

From that moment on, I absolutely adored that man – I couldn't do enough for him. And I told him as much on the way back to the airport when he said he had something for me.

'No, BB, please, it's been great to look after you, mate,' I said, 'it really has. Absolute pleasure.'

But he went to the boot of the car and as I hadn't been in back, I knew they must have sneaked something in there when I wasn't looking. And they had. They presented me with a signed photo – and I would never ask for anyone to sign anything while I was doing my job, so that was a rarity – and two bottles of wine. And they were *not* cheap, I can assure you. They were like a hundred pounds each.

'Those are for your wife,' he told me. 'Please send her my regards – and tell her she has a fine husband!'

Spats added, 'She probably already knows that, B!'

It was so thoughtful, so nice of them.

BB's presence stayed with me on the drive home. I reflected that he really didn't need to do any of those things, that his actions revealed his true character.

I never work for one person for longer than 12 weeks at a time. If the client still needs protection, I change the team, the whole team. You have to stay sharp to be an effective bodyguard, you have to stay fresh and if you get drawn into their world – which you do, no matter how long you spend with them – you can become over-familiar and then you lose your focus. That's why it's not good to stay too long, no matter how much they like you.

But if there was ever anyone about whom I thought, you know what? I'd love to stay with them forever, then it has to be BB King.

CHAPTER 24

ROY AND THE ROYALS

'What is this?' asked the Sheikha flatly. 'You don't like my money? Then why do you work for me?'

I had been accompanying the older sister of His Royal Highness Maktoum Al Maktoum on her daily walk when I said that maybe her assistant had given me too much money for running an errand. I thought I was doing her a favour. Wrong. It was a grave personal insult.

The sun continued to shine brightly, but the temperature in Hyde Park suddenly dropped a few degrees.

Why had I questioned her? Why?

As the Sheikha's representative on earth, her assistant essentially *was* the Sheikha. Question her judgement and you're telling off the most important woman in the Al Maktoum family. This, I may not need to tell you, is not a brilliant idea – I'm a fast learner, though.

'I'm awfully sorry, I do apologise, I didn't realise,' I said immediately. 'It will never happen again.'

'You may wait,' was the response. 'I will call you when I need you.'

She walked off alone and I realised that this wasn't just

a matter of protocol. I had upset her. Now I wasn't allowed to walk with her!

I'd never felt so bad in my life. What a mistake! And there was I thinking I was good at what I did and that I'd got it all covered. *And then you open your big, bloody mouth and put your fucking foot in it because you haven't done your homework!* Soon, I might well be out of a job.

A London company arranged security for key figures in the United Arab Emirates and for the King of Jordan. Their clients included the Al Maktoums, with whom I was working. Or at least, I *hoped* I was still working with them.

Their royal residence – what they would have called a 'palace' in their own country – took up all the houses in an upmarket London square. His Royal Highness Al Maktoum was one of the richest men in the world and had the Sheikha not been born a woman, she would have outranked her younger brother. As it was, in terms of esteem she was right up there and, nine times out of ten, he would go to her for advice.

Not only had I been asked to run her bodyguard detail, but I'd been assigned to look after her personally. Under me were 10 to 15 other bodyguards: the other members of the family and their children all needed protection. The families would stay in the UK between March and October or until the weather turned wintry and then they were off pretty sharpish.

Among her 25-strong entourage, the Sheikha had what I suppose you would call an equivalent of a lady-in-waiting – the personal assistant who had unwittingly got me into such trouble. She spoke very good English and went by an anglicised name – for her privacy I'll call her C.

C filled me in on some of the Arab royal protocol and each day, I greeted the Sheikha with 'Good morning, how are you?' in Arabic. It took me ages to get it right.

I could only look at the Sheikha when she spoke directly to me. Otherwise, I was to avoid her gaze out of deference to her rank and sex. For the same reason, she would always be fully veiled when we were out. Only her husband was allowed to see her face. In practice, as a bodyguard, I was a pretty intimate member of staff and I would see her without it but I always discreetly looked away.

I quite enjoy learning new rules and regulations. For example, I was never allowed to cross my feet in her presence – showing your soles is the equivalent of 'fuck off', and biting your fingernails means exactly the same thing.

When I got my charge to the park for her daily walk I always asked, as I opened the passenger door, 'Sheikha, am I required? Do you wish me to walk with you?'

She would reply, 'Yes,' and even though I knew she'd say that, I always had to ask in her world, a formal one of strict etiquette and a rigid hierarchy.

She walked with her ladies-in-waiting just behind her and I shadowed them on the left flank, with another guy behind me and two others mirroring us on the right – the bodyguard 'box formation'. We had to stay behind unless there was trouble when it was understood we had permission to move forward.

And do you know what the most common problem was? Abuse from passers-by. It makes me ashamed to be British to say that there are still people who will slag off a woman just because she's in traditional Arab dress. Unbelievable.

'*Look at them fucking wankers!*' And it wasn't just the chavs, but city suits too. '*State of her, who does she fucking think she is?*'

The Sheikha's regular position in the car was next to the left-hand door. Now that was one tradition that even I had a problem with; I always want the client behind me. If you want to get to her, you should have to go through me first. It felt like she would be unnecessarily exposed way over to the left, but no way! There was no chance that some British bodyguard was going to change royal protocol.

So C sat directly behind me and then there was what you might call the second lady-in-waiting who looked after the cash and she sat next to me. She always came shopping with us – and, let me tell you, the Arabs do love to shop: to the point that if the weather was bad, then their exercise would be an extended hike around Harrods of anything up to two hours.

The Sheikha would pick out what she wanted – 'that', 'that', '...and that' – and then the deputy lady-in-waiting made the purchase. It wasn't shopping as I knew it – most of it was in bulk, for a start. The Sheikha was extremely generous. If she bought one handbag, she'd usually buy ten. The others might be slightly lower quality, but they'd still be pretty nice and they would be distributed among her favoured staff.

The Sheikha paid for everything in cash, lots of cash, always £50 notes. No twenties. No tens and absolutely no fives. They just weren't interested in any other cash – and that was what got me in trouble.

I'd been told to collect a present that the Sheikha had picked out for her husband at the upmarket Fortnum & Mason. Because it was the Sheikha who had done the choosing, it had to be me who did the picking up. This was partly because there were strict rules about who could work for her and partly because if it was a gift from the Sheikha to her husband then it wasn't going to come cheap, even by their standards – and their standards were far from cost-cutting at the best of times.

Hubby was a prince and in all the months I worked with

the Sheikha he turned up a grand total of two times, but that had no bearing on the gift he would be given. C handed me an envelope stuffed with cash and asked me to bring back a receipt.

I called ahead to make sure that someone would be waiting at the Jermyn Street entrance to Fortnum & Mason, knowing that I wouldn't be able to find anywhere to park up, and then jumped into one of the family's Bentleys – gleaming white, brand-new, of course. The present was a beautiful, soft leather jacket and there was a member of staff waiting with it, just where I'd requested.

'That will be £3,500, sir,' he said. *Jesus Christ!* I thought. *No wonder this envelope's so thick!* So I tried to look as if I bought items like this for cash every day.

'Would you mind taking it out of that?' I said, as I handed over the envelope, 'and leave the receipt.' I took another look at the jacket. 'And can you place that on the front passenger seat.' *I'm bodyguarding the leather now!* I thought. *That's going nowhere!* I checked every inch of the garment, imagining the gruesome consequences if the Sheikha noticed a missing button.

Meanwhile, the sales guy was carefully counting the money – three times in all. He'd obviously done this before. He passed back the envelope. It was still loaded with fifties. I think I kept my eyes as much on the jacket as I did on the road all the way back. With some relief, I handed my precious cargo over to C.

'There you go, luv,' I said. 'There's the jacket there and here's the envelope with the rest of the money and the receipt.'

'No, no!' she said. 'Just the receipt! Thank you for going.'

What? The envelope was still stuffed was notes. *There must be some mistake.* There was. Only it was my mistake. I just couldn't believe they wouldn't want to hang on to so much cash. And it bothered me all day, holding this wad of notes. That's when I made the decision to mention it to the boss.

I knew exactly when the Sheikha would go for her walk that afternoon and, sure enough, she appeared right on cue and we took the usual ride to Hyde Park.

'May I ask you a question?' I said, as I opened the door for her. And that was when it all went wrong. I explained about the money and soon I was on my own in the park, kicking my arse all over the shop.

It must have been an hour or more before the Sheikha finally called for the car. I knew this was a crucial moment for my future with them. If I didn't want to be given the boot, I had to avoid grovelling – I must show that I could still be a proper man, a proper bodyguard, but without sounding rude.

'Shall I get the car, Sheikha?' I enquired politely.

'Yes, please.'

'Jolly good.'

I instructed one of the other bodyguards to pick up the car, just as I always did, and took her back as if nothing had happened. The atmosphere was calm, but definitely not friendly.

Not long afterwards, C got me on my own.

'Why did you ask her about the payment for the jacket?' she demanded.

'I wasn't sure... I didn't know the circumstances, but I wish you'd told me before,' I said. 'I'll never make the same mistake again but I know where I stand, so let's just carry on as we did before.'

I sounded decisive and I thought I'd played it right. She looked impressed and as she disappeared off to attend to the Sheikha, I sighed in relief to myself. I knew my position wasn't entirely secure again, but I was on my way back to being in favour.

C was all sunny and smiles the next day and the message was clear: the insult was forgotten, don't apologise again and don't mention it. She didn't, and I was careful not to either. The day's plan included, unsurprisingly, shopping.

'Lovely!' I said. 'Another handbag!'

She laughed at that; it was looking good.

Later in the morning I was given another errand. A more suspicious man than me might have thought this was a bit of a test – in fact, I'm sure it was.

'The Sheikha requires fresh toothpaste,' C informed me. 'She has a favourite brand from a particular chemist.' She gave me the details. Needless to say, the toothpaste was about five times the price of regular stuff. And, just as I had thought she would, C handed over the regulation £50 note. I had a feeling that I knew what was coming when I gave back the change and the receipt.

'No, no!' she said as before. 'Thank you for going.'

'Lovely!' I said, theatrically removing the notes from the envelope and giving her a big grin as I stuffed them in my back pocket. 'Nice few quid! That'll come in handy!' And when she laughed, I knew everything was going to be okay.

'*What?* You're not going to check?' she scolded me jokingly.

'You have got to be kidding,' I said. 'That's *mine*!' I rubbed my hands by way of comic emphasis.

She took the toothpaste to the Sheikha and a minute or two later I heard laughter from upstairs as C relayed the story. She must have gone straight in there and told her boss that the Englishman had finally got it.

But the Sheikha was still testing me out when she got in the car that lunchtime.

'Mr Roy, we are going shopping,' she said firmly.

'Yeah, I know, Sheikha,' I said, 'I've got a few quid meself for Harrods!' I could see in the mirror that she almost had to bite her own lip to keep from laughing – she couldn't be seen to be sharing a joke with a man. But her smirk said it all. She quickly rattled off something in Arabic to C, who laughed again – and so did the other lady-in-waiting next to me. I had no idea what it was all about, but it seemed like I'd done okay.

It was when we got back that C asked to speak to me in private. We went out to the back of the house, to a room usually reserved for meetings of the ladies of the house.

'The Sheikha wishes for you to be with her right through until the end of her stay.'

So I had passed my probation but C wasn't finished.

'Today, in the car, we were talking…'

'Yes, and it was at my expense,' I told her.

'The Sheikha said, "I like this man. I do not think he ever makes the same mistake twice. And I like his sense of humour, he makes me laugh. But you must tell him, he must stop making me laugh. It is against the rules."'

'You know what?' I said. 'That's one rule I will never abide by!'

'We are going to have fun working with you, Roy,' laughed C. 'We like you!' And then, almost without a break she completely changed her tone. 'Now, a serious point: Neil, Mark, Ian...' she said, referring to the other bodyguards who had been provided. 'The Sheikha does not like them; she does not wish to see them again. Get rid of them!'

Bang! That was it, from a shared joke to a mass sacking in a sentence. The Al Maktoum family didn't mess about.

The rest of my time with the Sheikha ran totally smoothly, until it came to Ascot. She had learned she was pregnant and Arab women aren't allowed to leave the house at all for the first month or so. I was asked to take His Highness Maktoum Al Maktoum instead.

His Highness's place was out in Richmond Park. I can't think of many other people who would be allowed to buy 65 acres of the Park to graze livestock but then he is the biggest single racing horse owner in the world. There was one race at Ascot in which every entrant was his, every single one. He even had one of the entrances to the Park blocked off to the public to maintain private access to his grounds.

'Hello, Mr Roy,' said Maktoum Al Maktoum when he got in the car.

'Good morning, your Royal Highness.'

'We go to Ascot today.'

'Yes, your Highness.'

'You know what day it is today?'

'Yes...' and I reeled off the date.

'No, no,' he laughed. 'At the races?'

'Er, no.'

'It is...' he said, with *Carry On* relish, '*Ladies Day!*'

As he laughed, I could see the glint in his eye. I thought, *I'm going to like this fella.* Like his sister, he had a Bentley, but I was surprised when he insisted on sitting in front next to me. I soon guessed it was his usual position; he wasn't the tallest man in the world and when he pressed a button, the specially modified passenger seat rose up until he was at my level. Anyone watching as we drove along would have thought he was an absolute giant.

He loved his gadgets. The car was custom-built and it was just full of buttons and dials in the front of it. *Me?* I just drove the damn car – he was forever fiddling and messing around.

'What does this do?'

'Stop it!' I mock-ordered, which his two senior servants sitting in the back found very amusing. The man himself played along all the way till we got through the gates.

'Mr Roy, Mr Roy, *look!*' he called out. He indicated outside the car towards the elegantly dressed women, but I don't think he had one in particular in mind when he breathed, '*Got big breasts...*'

'Behave yourself!' I told him.

The fun stopped the second we got out of the car. At once he was the dignified royal personage and I was the stone-faced bodyguard. You wouldn't have thought we had ever exchanged a word, much less ogled birds all the way in. It was still hard to stifle a smile, though, because once out of the car, he was suddenly about a foot shorter than me.

We marched into his VIP tent and he dismissed me almost immediately. For a second I was concerned, thinking I was leaving him alone, but then I noticed two massive blokes, one on each side of the room in full ceremonial gear, headdress and everything. They weren't part of his family – he had his own personal bodyguards. I knew he was well protected and so I ambled out to the car.

The Al Maktoums had put a lot of money into a particular London hospital and so I was surprised when the Sheikha elected to go to The Portland Hospital for the birth. It was only later that I discovered the other hospital was reserved for the males in the family. As it was, news quickly spread of the imminent arrival among the sizeable family and the corridors, entrance and grounds of the hospital were packed with well-wishers.

I knew that I would only be permitted to travel so far with her and then she would be taken on by her female staff. I was just a fella, not to mention a bodyguard and a Westerner. That suited me fine and I nipped outside for a fag. Typical Roysie!

No sooner had I sparked up than her brother's big, white

The London Television Centre Upper Ground London SE1 9TT
Telephone 020 7827 7000 Facsimile 020 7827 7001 www.gmtv.co.uk

Date: 20.07.2002

Dear Roy,

I would like to express my great gratitude to you and Personal Protection Promotions for protecting me in what could have proved to be a very volatile situation.

The job you had to do was a difficult one – it called for a cool head yet a sharp ability to be aware of any signs that I could have been in danger.

Thanks to you and Personal Protection Promotions I was allowed to move home and remain safe.

You and your colleague Ron Killick acted with confidence and wonderful professionalism. You were both true gentleman.

You did an amazing job. Thank you so much Roy, Ron and everyone at PPP.

Lots of love and gratitude!

Anne O'Neill

I like to think I was not bad at my job – what do you think?

Above left: If there was one man I would have stayed with permanently this is him; I absolutely adored him.

Above right: My signed Meat Loaf book. What a character!

Below: Me with two Special Forces guys at the training camp. Once you go through those gates your whole world changes, believe me.

Above: Always professional at all times, you made me so proud. What a team.

Below: Transporting someone is never a problem; stay out of our way please!

Above: His Royal Highness the King of Jordan's private jet and card.

Below: At the bottom of the plane's steps, he presented me with a gold watch to thank me for being his personal bodyguard. I would like to say thank you, Your Royal Highness.

Above left: Me with Vinnie Jones and Alan Ford (don't we look well!)

Above right: On set with the late Mike Reid – the greatest comedian and actor, sadly missed.

Below: Time to carve up Sunday lunch (only joking!)

Above: My darling wife Jo Jo on our wedding day (someone was shining down on her that day).

Below: Me and Jo Jo on our wedding day, 27th August 1994 (love you so much my darling).

Above: My beautiful darling daughters, Victoria and Eden – Daddy loves you so much.

Below: With my little princess, Eden (Daddy's girl).

The oil painting presented to me by Universal Music – artist Sindy Belle – thank you so much.

Bentley purred into the car park. The fag went straight out the other side of my mouth and I stood tall as I could, arse out, shoulders back.

'Your Highness,' I nodded over his head as he came towards me.

'Ah! Mr Roy. Walk with me.'

I hadn't expected that. The corridors were lined both sides with family and friends, every inch. All eyes flickered towards me as I made my return with Al Maktoum. Nobody could believe that I was allowed to accompany him. Nor could I, for that matter!

Through the set of double doors from which I'd just been turned back and into the maternity unit itself...

We were walking side by side when Al Maktoum casually flicked his prayer beads over my thumb. It was a mark of the highest accord. I'd never felt so emotional in my life: it meant that I'd become part of his family. It still chokes me now to think about it.

He took me to the very doors of the delivery room. In terms of protocol, it was a complete no-no to be that close to the royal sister. Maktoum stopped and turned, and I faced him. I could feel the gaze of everyone else in the room behind me burning into my back.

'Mr Roy,' he said gravely. 'You stand... *here*.' As he said the words, he took my right hand to his mouth and kissed it just once.

Everyone we'd passed would have died just to be standing where I was. And as he disappeared into the delivery room – that was his prerogative as her brother – I thought to myself, *if looks could kill, Roysie, you'd be a dead man!*

He soon returned with a broad smile, saying, 'We have joy, we must celebrate! *Walk with me*.' Then he started talking quickly in Arabic to the throng waiting to congratulate him all the way back to the car.

I had a moment to recover myself as he was driven away and then C appeared from behind me.

'Mr Roy, I hear what happened,' she said quietly. 'How do you feel?' She knew.

I blinked, and tears came down my face. She took my hand and she wiped my face as I leant forward. She smiled. 'You don't have to speak,' she said. 'I understand. You can go now. You go home, you go to your family.'

And she was right: I probably couldn't have carried on. The emotion just took over. *The honour they bestowed on me...* You might not get that in a lifetime.

I had to pull myself together when I got home and I told the story to my missus.

'*And?*' said Joanne. That brought me back down to earth! I quickly realised that the story wouldn't mean that much to most people who didn't know the culture.

It had all been so intense that when they flew back, I was looking forward to taking a bit of a break. I thought I'd have a few weeks off, but almost immediately I got another call. My name had been passed round the Arab community as a result of the success I'd had with the Al Maktoums.

The results were a bit mixed – some families thought I'd got too close and viewed me with suspicion. Others thought I would be more trustworthy – for exactly the same reasons.

And one of them requested that I join him in Scotland and head up his bodyguard detail while he was in the UK.

'*Scotland?*' I asked.

'Yeah!' they told me. 'But this one's a short gig. It's a turnaround trip because they're coming over culling.'

I didn't get the chance to ask any more details. The boss would never reveal details of a job over an unsecured telephone line. If I wanted to hear more, I would have to go in and talk to him about it.

I was to be away for just seven days and that suited me just fine – ideally I'd prefer to be going home at the end of the night, but I was certainly intrigued.

The largest independent landowner in Scotland was His Royal Highness King Abdullah bin Al Hussein – the King of Jordan – and he was bringing over a shooting party. The 65,000 acres in the royal pad had been unoccupied for two years and in the interim the Highland deer on his estate had got on with the business of extending their families with commendable dedication. I was to look after everyone and was responsible for all the weaponry.

But my first stop was the garage to pick up the vehicles for the trip. This being the King of Jordan, you won't be surprised to learn it wasn't a lock-up with a couple of old Volvos. They had a massive storage facility based in south London, though you wouldn't know from the outside that the anonymous building was an automotive heaven.

One of the three – *three* – floors was given over solely to Ferraris and Porsches. Above that were Mercedes limos, which were used by the ladies to take the kids shopping. I headed for the top floor, past rows of Bentleys and Rolls-Royces, to a covered area tucked away at the back. The staff had been expecting me and one of them pulled off the sheets.

Waiting for us underneath was a grand total of four gleaming monsters. *Humvees!* And I mean proper, armour-plated, fully-loaded Humvees. Top-of-the-range, custom designed, close protection transportation: the genuine article. Bomb-proof, bullet-proof... the whole works. And it wasn't left-hand drive, or right-hand. You climbed up inside and took your place in the *centre* of the vehicle, flanked by another bloke each side.

I don't know how much those motors cost but they couldn't have been less than £250,000 each. And they did about seven miles to the gallon.

The following morning my team began the 18-hour journey which would take us from London to the Highlands. Each of the four drivers had a gold credit card laid out on his dashboard, good in most petrol stations. The one-way trip was £925 per Humvee...

As I pulled in the lead vehicle, it was with relief that I saw the sign welcoming us to Glasgow. *Lovely!* I thought to myself. *Scotland, at last!* But then I looked at the map in detail and realised that Glasgow to where we were going was nearly the same distance again. And the hardest part was still to come: from then on the roads got very twisty, turning and mountainous as we inched our way into the Highlands. All the while I was straining to make sure I didn't accidentally cull any deer – it would have been rather embarrassing to take out one of the King's prize specimens before he had a chance to shoot it.

The Royal house was a former hotel which you might think would be easy to spot, but for the King discretion was everything and he'd chosen a place that was tucked away in the Highlands – so tucked away that we almost couldn't find the thing!

We were the advance party and eventually we arrived in the middle of the night at a hotel right up in the Highlands. The team was absolutely knackered, but the only sign of life was a single light in the foyer. In a heightened state brought on by exhaustion, the scrubby, bare landscape seemed particularly windswept and desolate. The building loomed about as invitingly as that pub the two backpackers find in *An American Werewolf in London*. Just one fella sat in the dingy gloom of the reception.

'Hello, lads,' he said in the broadest Scottish accent us London lads had ever heard. 'We've been waiting for you for quite a while now.' I cracked up, half-expecting him to warn us to beware of the moon and stick to the paths.

The next morning, I almost thought I'd woken up on a different planet. In the bright sunlight, I drank in the fresh air, had a fag and stared into the distance at a beautiful range of mountains. Beautiful. It was breathtaking scenery, quite stunning. I took loads of photos. But we were also there to do a job.

I perched myself back in the centre of the Humvee, got it roaring into life and we juddered slowly and uneconomically all the way back down the path again.

The landscape stretched out in front of us without a sign of any human habitation for ages, but then it seemed as if a huge building was rising out of the ground. The King's palace! I realised that the old hotel had been sited so that it was completely undetectable from the road we'd just been on. He could get on with things there without people coming up all the time to have a gawp.

The King of Jordan's security was headed by a very grand colonel-in-chief with all the pips and everything. If any of us made a mistake and upset him, we'd be off! It was as simple as that.

We were busy from the moment we arrived. One of the first visitors to the King's house was the chief local policeman – in Scotland, they call them the sheriff. He was there about those frisky deer. Their numbers were strictly regulated by law and the King's had gone way over their allocation in the two years that the place had been empty.

The sheriff brought a magistrate with him. It was a serious business – I heard later that the King had to pay a whopping fine, though I guess it was small change to him. But the sheriff got his cheque in double-quick time and practically skipped off to the car.

I was asked to pick up some of the King's guests for the week's festivities. There were a couple of helicopters in the grounds but I guess these visitors weren't that highly ranked because the nearest airport was a two-and-a-half hour drive from the house. In the arrivals hall were some fellas who looked like they were also bodyguards and I wondered if they were part of the same party.

'Roy Snell,' I said to one of them, showing my ID. He confirmed that he was also in security. 'Are you for the same group as us?'

'No, we've got just one bloke who's coming over by helicopter. He's here to climb Ben Nevis. Funnily enough, he's just coming through now.'

He gestured towards the arrivals door as none other than Steven Seagal sauntered through. We got chatting and he revealed that he started his own career as a bodyguard. I only needed to say that my clients were being picked up for United Emirates and he understood immediately. He told me that he'd fallen in love with Kelly LeBrock when she was one of his clients and, like me, he didn't believe in crossing the line so he gave up the job and became an actor. She financed his first film, *Nico*.

Much later that night, I arrived back at the house with my guests. I was pretty tired by then and just wanted to get their luggage unloaded. A light went on above the side door and I was out immediately, dragging the cases to the door – I was particularly eager because that would mean our end of the job would be done for the night and I could get some much-needed kip. There was a bloke waiting by the door and he smiled a greeting.

'All right, mate, lovely,' I said gratefully. 'Cop hold of that one...' He took each case and disappeared inside with them, before returning without a word for the next.

By the third trip to the door the Colonel had emerged and stood staring directly at me. *Why's he looking at me?* He put a hand discreetly to one side of his face and mouthed something at me. *What'd he say?* No time, I was desperate to finish off and give the last load to the helpful fella who'd been taking it inside. The Colonel looked quite anxious now. What was he muttering? Then I realised. '*King!*' he was saying. '*King!*'

I stopped dead in my tracks. The bloke who'd been taking the cases from me came out again: plain white shirt. Jeans. Ordinary shoes.

'Are you Mr Roy?' he asked.

'Yes...' I said, a little hesitantly.

'Nice to meet you,' he said politely.

The Colonel cleared his throat, then said, 'May I introduce the King of Abu Dhabi?'

I'd been giving him the bags! If the ground could have swallowed me up... but he'd never said anything. I just thought he was one of the man servants. You can imagine what was being said in my earpiece. The guys were chattering away to each other. 'Yeah, we ain't gotta worry about the King's bags...' 'Yeah, he carries them himself, doesn't he?' 'Yeah, guv, don't you worry yourself about them...'

It just goes to show: no matter how good you think you are, you can always make a mistake.

But the rest of the week went without a hitch and then came an incredible moment, one that I will never forget. We got the royal party to the plane for their onward trip to New York and just before they boarded, the King of Jordan barked out an order in Arabic to one of his aides, who disappeared into the aircraft. I took the opportunity to approach the King.

'Your Highness, it's been a pleasure...' I began.

'No, no, the pleasure has been all mine,' he interrupted. 'Mr Roy, I have a small gift for you.'

The aide ran back down the stairs of the plane and presented me with a wrapped box.

'I've had this specially made for you in Switzerland to thank you from the bottom of my heart.'

Inside was a beautiful, 24-carat, sold gold watch with a crocodile strap, engraved with the King's emblem. I was taken aback by his generosity; I really hadn't expected anything. I knew I'd done my job, one hundred per cent, but the honour afforded by the formal kiss on the cheek would have been enough.

It made me think again of how much criticism of the Arabs there is in the UK. Yet if people made the effort to get to know them, they would understand a lot more about respect; that your effort and hard work is always appreciated.

However, I was still relieved that the week's work was almost over. It was going to be a long trip. We'd rumbled as far as Cardiff in Wales when the phone went. It was the London office and they sounded tense.

'Have you heard?'

'*What?*' I asked.

They asked where we were and sounded none too happy at the answer.

'Hm...' they said. 'Next service station, pull over. You might be going back.'

London... Joanne... No! I tried to get them to tell me what was going on.

'Put the radio on,' they said, then hung up. Steve was in the vehicle directly behind me. He started flashing his lights at me. This was getting really strange. What the fuck was going on? I reached for the radio.

The date was 11 September 2001. The first plane had just hit the Twin Towers and the King of Jordan was somewhere over the Atlantic.

As the news relayed the chaos in the US, one thing was clear: nobody was safe from the fallout, not even the King of Jordan. America had gone into lockdown and it seemed highly likely that his plane would be turned around, in which case we would have to be there waiting for him when he returned.

We waited, as instructed, in the car park of the service station for more than an hour. I snatched up the phone before it had finished its first ring.

'Gentlemen, carry on home. The job is finished. They've been diverted to Jordan.'

Yes! I was going back to south London, back to my family! I even took a few days off before I got back out with the royals. But this time, it wasn't the Arabs.

I was asked to do the security at Buckingham Palace for Princess Alice's 100th birthday party. She was a popular lady and so there were hundreds of guests, all with their vehicles. Things started off well – I got all the guests into the Palace in just 55 minutes. But that wasn't good enough for me; I was determined to beat the time. This would be a game of matching up the right people to the right cars and it was made slightly more complicated by not knowing what order people would come out. I got two top boys on the job and I managed to clear Princess Alice's guests in 38 minutes.

The chief inspector of the Royal protection squad arrived and had a brief conference just inside the ground with the head butler and Prince Philip – who soon came over to me.

'Ah, Mr Snell,' said His Royal Highness. 'May I say what a good job you've done here this evening...'

As he left, I was approached by the Chief Inspector.

'I've seen some people do D-bus and E-bus in my time,' he said, with a knowing smile. I realised he knew the business and grinned back at him as he continued, 'but by your stature and the way you presented yourself and the way you've organised yourself, I'd say you've been in the game for a while. You've done an extremely good job. I really appreciate the time and effort you've put in.'

'Thanks very much,' I said. Coming from him, that was nice.

A few months later, I ran into him when I covered the VIP section in Blenheim Palace during a performance by the Royal Philharmonic. Instantly, he recognised me.

'Mr Snell!' he said. 'Now I know the evening will run smoothly!'

'Thanks for the vote of confidence,' I said.

He turned to his colleague and said, 'This gentleman here *really* knows his stuff. We've worked together before, haven't we, Mr Snell?'

'Yes, we have,' I replied.

'We had a *lovely* evening in Buckingham Palace, I can assure you,' he continued, before discussing the arrangements for the evening with me. The Royal Protection Squad themselves took in the members of the family such as Princess Anne, while I followed up close behind, thinking to myself, *Only I could do this, being part of the entourage for the Royal Family!*

It could only happen to me and it was such a lovely evening – I thoroughly enjoyed that concert because I had a perfect seat: at the front.

CHAPTER 25

THE AMERICANS

Carol Vorderman soon realised what kind of character she was dealing with. I'd picked her up at a hotel and she said, 'You must be Roy. Are you with me all night?'

'If you like, darlin', yeah!' I said. It was just a joke to break the ice.

'Oh I *see*!' she said. 'I've got one here, haven't I?'

My business was building up to the point where I could barely keep up with the stream of names that I was now dealing with. Whenever we did award ceremonies, there might be dozens of major celebrities. I next met Carol at the TV Awards at the Royal Albert Hall in 2000. Everyone who was anyone was there and it seemed that we were driving them all. I'd assigned Carol to myself, and the lads were all joshing me about how I'd managed to get her.

But that was just the start of an incredibly busy day.

Carol was safely seated in the Awards and said she'd probably stay for the aftershow party. That gave me just enough time to nip across town to Wembley, to assist a pal who was working with Britney Spears. I already knew Britney's US bodyguards, Big Rob and Big Chris, from the circuit. Their nicknames might as well have both been 'massive' – and from someone my size, that's saying something! Those two are absolutely *huge*. I remember that Christine Aguilera had a couple of guys who were even larger – for a while celebrities seemed to be trying to outdo each other with extra-large size security. Didn't make much sense to me: the bigger they are, the slower they move. You might be in trouble if they catch you, but chances are you can out-manoeuvre them and they won't have a hope in hell.

Still, it didn't matter how big you were in the UK – if you were an American bodyguard, you were not allowed to work over here without some of the local lads. And that's where I came in.

I'd hardly got to the venue before the call came through that Carol had decided to make her own way home, which freed me up for Britney: a lovely lass, a real sweetheart. We got on really well, but it wasn't until the third day I realised just how at home her own security was feeling.

'You know what?' Big Chris told me. 'We're gonna take today off – we're going sight-seeing!'

Although I laughed, I also knew how much that really meant – they realised she was in safe hands.

I left Ronnie to it while I dealt with logistics for security for US country singers Faith Hill and Tim McGraw.

'We've had to close down a tattooist in Covent Garden,' Ronnie called me to report, 'in the basement level of the market. I had to go in there and check it out for her – she wanted a tattoo on her bum.'

'Someone gets all the jobs, don't they?'

'Yeah!' he said. 'There's Britney Spears, arse in the air and there's me standing right next to her.'

'What was the tattoo?'

'Oh, I dunno,' he replied. 'I never looked!'

The US clients were on their way. Tim McGraw regularly sells out 50,000-seat arenas over in the States. His wife Faith was releasing an album called *Breathe* and Steve Margo, senior vice-president at Warner Music, had called to ask my firm to do the full security for a round of promotion throughout Europe. I'd be with them for the full 21 days and I sighed, thinking about all the work ahead, as I flicked through what they called the 'manifest' – the running order of what they're going to be doing, where they're going and where they were appearing, which included a chat with Johnny Vaughan on his evening show.

I remembered Johnny from when I happened to be in a club that he was relaxing in. Maybe a bit too much – I had to help him out and into a cab a bit lively!

Faith and Tim brought over the whole family, complete with nanny and teacher for the kids. I had to ensure the safety of them all. And I also had to find a house – they thought it would be better to rent a place rather than settle for the impersonal surroundings of some anonymous hotel.

Back home they had a beautiful place and it took us a while to find something that would keep them in the style to which they had become accustomed: a beautiful, secluded place buried somewhere in Oxfordshire. The journey to London was doable – just zip up the A40. Tim would simply get on with his own thing and look after the kids. They were such a close family, loving and god-fearing; I really did adore them. We struck up a very close relationship – or at least as close as I would allow it to be. Always keep the edge of professional distance.

Ronnie was our advance party. I flew with the family in one of their two jets – his'n'hers – and he'd meet us on the tarmac with cars that he'd arranged locally. We got into a routine which was only broken when he pointed out another plane parked up nearby, a massive great thing. It was the focal point for frantic activity.

'Take a look,' said Ronnie. I squinted against the sunlight. And then I realised – Air Force One. We'd been held above the airport for an extra hour that day and now I knew why; that plane had a solid ring of security men. And quite a few of them seemed to be keeping their beady eyes trained in our direction. I'm glad I didn't fart, sneeze or shit – they were a jittery bunch and I reckon they'd have shot us as soon as said anything!

We did two or more countries most days; customs handled wherever the couple's jet stopped rather than them having to go through the airport. Handy. But what a dizzying ride! I remember Joanne phoned me when we were out in Spain and I had to think for a moment before I could tell her what country I was in, let alone the name of the town.

There was only one awkward moment with the family during the whole of the trip. Faith was walking in front of Tim and me, and he drawled, 'Say, Roy, could I ask you a question?'

'Of course you can, Tim.'

'Do you think my wife's got a good ass?'

That's a bit of a question. If I say no, I thought, *I'm in trouble. But if I say yes, it'll be even worse. It's a no-win situation.*

'*Oi!*' I said. 'What do you mean?'

'Ahm just wondering...why you keep looking at it.'

But I was looking in front of her, at the side where she was walking; I was looking for potential problems. I didn't have the time or, frankly, the inclination to be booty-checking.

'I can assure you,' I said firmly, 'I am *not* ogling your

wife's "arse". I am looking ahead – and if you look where I'm looking, you will see I am looking ahead and *not* at your wife.'

'You know what?' he said, after a moment. 'Even I can make mistakes. Sorry, buddy.'

Tim took his jet back a few days early to play a tour in the States. As we did the airport transfer, Faith took the opportunity to say, 'I have never, ever felt so safe in all my life. You really, really know your stuff!'

She nearly had *me* in bleedin' tears, the cow-bag! She was so appreciative, but you know they were both such nice people in every sense that even if I hadn't been working, I just would have wanted to protect them.

CHAPTER 26

THEY CALL ME MR SNELL

Bodyguards for *chess players*? Surely this must be a wind-up! The World Championships were televised from the studios in Hammersmith and simultaneously broadcast on the Internet to allow viewers to interact with the games. My job was to ensure there wasn't any interference in the progress of the matches.

I was assigned to reigning champion Garry Kasparov and every morning he and opponent Vladimir Kramnik were scanned for bugs, earpieces and skulduggery – as was everyone else who came to the tournament. I thought this was all very strange and I sensed some kind of rather sinister undercurrent to the set-up.

The games seemed to go okay – I don't know the rules of chess in detail but it looked like it came down to some kind of stand-off between the two players. Play was stopped altogether on one of the last days and it was all getting rather tense. I called in to see the woman who ran the promotional company.

'How are things?' I asked. She seemed rather upset.

'I'm not sure what's going on,' she admitted, 'but

something's not right. There is a lot of money changing hands in the betting. We think it's something to do with the Russian mafia.'

My first instinct was to go *whoa, whoa, whoa!* That's a big conclusion to jump to. The organisers warned one of the guys in the auditorium might have been feeding information somewhere – and of course all the journalists desperately wanted there to be some kind of criminal Russian connection. I half-wondered if it might not all have been press speculation. Everyone was getting jumpy. Even my guys were becoming a bit anxious at the thought of who might be out there.

'Listen,' I told them, 'we're not going to take any notice of what people are saying until we get known facts. Until you hear it from me directly, you just carry on as normal. Let's not carried away.'

Nevertheless, I was asked to make the suspect man close down his laptop. The media loved it. They thought it was hilarious that I escorted this bloke – seven-stone dripping wet – from the building. Immediately they christened me 'Knuckles' and tried to get some kind of story out of me. But I wasn't going to speak out of turn and I didn't know anything, anyway. And I certainly wasn't 'Knuckles'!

'Look, as you can see, we're not thugs,' I said. 'We wear suits – we don't wear tracksuits and T-shirts, d'ya know what I mean? We're a professional outfit. We try to do everything in a professional manner. But don't let the suits and everything fool you – it's not that we can't handle ourselves, because I can assure you that if the shit hits the fan, we can turn.'

'Yeah,' said the journalist. 'I've been watching you for the last few days. I was a rascal in my day, but I can tell you... you scare the *shit* out of me!'

Then I remembered where I'd seen the fella before. It was John McVicar – armed bank robber-turned-writer. He put most of what we'd talked about into print, adding, 'Mr Snell points out that he wears a suit, shirt and tie. If I remember correctly, so did the Krays.'

I laughed when I read this. *Yeah, if only you knew, Mr McVicar – I married their niece!*

The rest of the tournament passed without incident, though I seem to remember that Kasparov lost his title. It was about two months later that I read a story alleging that the finance for the whole show had come from the mafia. I have no idea if that's true but it does go to show that sometimes the most straightforward gig can turn out to have a bit of an edge.

If chess audiences had a reputation for restraint, the same couldn't be said of Will Young, who had won the first *Pop Idol* and quickly went on to release an album, which he promoted at the Virgin Megastore in the West End. They got me in because they thought the hysteria might soon get out of hand. No problem – an easy day's graft. Will himself was a nice enough young man and, just as I thought, it wasn't hard to deal with the screaming fans.

I scanned the queue while he signed autographs and noticed a young girl in a wheelchair. The star had to take a break because his wrist hurt from all the writing. He was gone for about 15 minutes – I think he was probably having tea and cakes to make his hand feel better, the poor love – and the girl was still waiting. Now she was looking a bit upset. I went over and asked her mum what was up.

'Well, it doesn't look like we'll get an autograph,' she said. 'But I understand because I know he's very busy. It's just that she's followed him all the way through and she's a big fan.'

'Are you here to get your stuff signed?' I asked. 'Is that what you want?'

'Yes,' said the girl.

'Okay. Well, just bear with me one moment.'

I went up to where Will was seated and told the people at the front to hang on.

'Will, can I have a word?'

'What's the matter?' he asked.

So I told him what was going on and I'll give the boy his due, he said, 'Certainly, Mr Snell.'

Will Young was typical of a lot of the newer acts I was beginning to see. My reputation preceded me and now they wouldn't call me Roy. It was 'Mr Snell' or 'Sir'.

Will immediately went across to the girl and signed all her memorabilia. He even gave her a free copy of his CD and had his photograph taken with her. I thought that was a wonderful gesture. I love things like that – that's the way celebrities should be.

I was busier than I had ever been. Lots of acts were asking after me personally – Blue, Westlife... I was even called on for the last gig at the old Wembley Stadium before it was pulled down. The venue was to go out in style, turning up the rock'n'roll to maximum for a performance by Oasis in front of 50,000 fans.

I'd been asked to take Shaznay Lewis of All Saints and a few of her friends to the aftershow party. I thought it would be even easier than the Will Young gig – pick the girls up, let them watch the gig, have a bit of a party and then back home. How wrong can you be? Somehow, I always jump the gun.

The party was in a huge hall behind the stadium itself. Everyone was having a lovely time and the place was packed with celebrities – not only from the rock world, but actors too. One of the band's security men approached me to ask if the girls were coming up to 'say hello'. Unknown to me – and the rest of the world – at the time, Liam Gallagher was seeing Natalie from All Saints. You could see how much they were in love – *Jesus! She was like a little puppy: she adored him. Couldn't wait to go upstairs to the inner sanctum and see him.*

From my professional point of view, I was very impressed with the security around Oasis. Very tight, they had a good operation.

'Ah! Big fella,' said Liam when he saw me. 'How are ya, Mr Snell?'

I'd never met him. I said, 'I see my name is getting about.'

'Yeah,' said Liam. 'It certainly is. We should have a little chat later.'

What was on Liam's mind was Oasis when they were off-duty. The brothers would often be seeing their respective partners and he asked me to do close protection for both of them.

I took them to studios, drove them around and one thing I will say about them is that they were always respectful – both lads called me 'Sir'. They would not call me 'Roy', would not call me 'Mr Snell', just 'Sir'. Especially Liam. And I think Noel half-liked that.

If he gets out of hand, I'll get Roy. I was proud of where I'd got to in my industry.

It was a crying shame when Noel's marriage to Meg broke down. I got on well with her too and I never took sides. Noel was spaced out by the split. His expression reminded me of my feelings during my own marriage breakdown and what I'd thought about the daughter in the middle of it all.

'If you keep thinking about it constantly, young man,' I said, into the rear-view mirror, 'you're going to drive yourself mad.' He'd been slumped in misery and now he looked up and met my gaze sharply, as if wondering, *How the fuck does he know what I'm thinking?*

I continued: 'You're not the only one who's gone through this. I know exactly what's going through your mind at the moment. It's about the child, it's about the missus, it's about the split, it's about the cost... and don't tell me it isn't, because it is.'

And I think that impressed him, in the sense that I must have hit three out of four of his worries in one shot. He opened up and we became close – though I still always maintained some distance, even then.

Never cross the line.

I stayed in contact with Meg until they had sorted their split and after that I wasn't really needed. But I was touched when Meg kept in touch even after that; we just hit it off. There was no attraction there – my heart and my soul are devoted to my wife – but we got on. There was no crap between us. She knew not to ask me about Noel and I would never break her confidence to him. That was a special friendship.

I even got to see their daughter grow up for a few years. And it was good to see Meg stop her partying lifestyle, get a radio gig and some magazine work, and really turn herself around. She became a fitness fanatic. And she was a really sweet, lovely lady.

CHAPTER 27

A PINT WITH BRAD

I'd wanted to break into doing close protection for movie stars and so when I heard that a film was being shot in and around London, I jumped at the opportunity to wedge my big foot in the door. Me and Ronnie went along to see the production company and did the whole pitch. We told them the clients we supplied and the services we provided, but what I didn't know was the woman we were talking to was the casting director of the film and she had something different in mind for me. She was staring at the pair of us thoughtfully.

'Would you mind holding on for a minute?' she asked, then stood up.

'Not at all,' I said.

I looked at Ronnie, all the while thinking, *we're in here, son, we've got a chance here!*

Soon she returned with *Lock, Stock and Two Smoking Barrels* director Guy Ritchie.

'Do you see what I mean?' she said to him.

'Yeah,' he said, looking closely at us. *At me!* 'Definitely. *Definitely!* Hundred per cent.' With that, he walked out of the door.

That's handy! I thought – *we've definitely got the contract*.

'We'd like to offer you a part in the movie,' she smiled.

'*Sorry?*' I spluttered. 'I'm not an actor...'

'Yeah, we know. But we just want you to play yourself.'

'No, no, no,' I said quickly. 'I'm not doing films! I'm not an actor.'

But it wouldn't be the first time I'd been in front of the cameras. In 2000, when the fella playing *EastEnders'* Big Ron died, they asked me to do his storyline. Big Roy.

'We'd like you to do that gravel voice,' the director said. 'You know the one, when you get slightly...'

'You mean *that voice*?' I growled menacingly.

'That's the one.'

Barbara Windsor and Martin Kemp both pushed the idea. I just busked it, but afterwards, Martin asked me, 'Where did you train, then?'

'I've never been to drama school in my life!'

He was impressed: 'Well, you're a bloody natural! Absolute natural.'

So I assume Guy Ritchie's casting director thought the same thing. Something must have been there. That's how I got to play alongside Brad Pitt in *Snatch*.

And not to forget it meant I was paid twice – once for doing the security and then again for a bit of acting. Nice touch.

I also got to meet some of the other cast and crew – Dennis Farina, who was in *Crime Story*, and Mike Reid, who I also knew from *EastEnders*.

Mike and I were chatting in his caravan and, as he took his shirt off to change, he reached into the wardrobe. Nothing there! He stopped.

'You know what, Roysie?' he said. 'I think we need to go next door.'

'Whaddya mean?'

'We're in the wrong fucking caravan!' he roared. He was a super fella.

But I was mainly working with Alan Ford, who played Brick Top. I was the main heavy, dishing out the punishment. I suppose I couldn't have expected anything else. Guy Ritchie would forever be asking me stuff like, 'Is this how you garrotte someone, Roy?'

'What you asking me for?'

And then the shotgun: 'Is this what a sawn-off really looks like, Roy?'

'*Whaddya keep asking me for?*' I joked, pretending to be annoyed. 'Why is it that every time you want to kill someone, shoot someone, stab someone – you keep coming to *me*?'

But Guy got his own back: he killed me three times. First, I was shot in the front seat of a Jag. Blood, bullet hole, *cut*! Lovely. A week later I was garrotted in the same car, pulled out and strangled. I got a round of applause that time, which was quite nice. And then I was called back for the final scene, which made it into the movie. Now I knew why actors complain all time about having to hang around in the acting game – there's an awful lot of waiting. Even so, I had a lovely time. Everyone from Brad Pitt down, every single one was a pleasure to spend time with.

Brad confided that he'd always wanted to have a pint in an English pub. Unlike anyone else working abroad, he couldn't go anywhere without a huge entourage. I suggested we go five or six miles down the road where they didn't know about the movie to find a little country boozer. Ronnie would drive us.

There were only 20 or so people in our chosen venue and most of them were quite elderly, nursing their half of

Guinness for the afternoon. But for Brad Pitt it was a huge novelty. *Normality!* You'd have thought that man had won the Lottery as I ordered up a couple of pints of lager for me and Ronnie and a Guinness for the world's biggest movie star. He excitedly phoned Jennifer Aniston to tell her that he was in a pub in England. Meanwhile, none of the customers had a clue about him.

The barman, however, had twigged something was going on and kept looking over at us. I didn't want to push our luck, so as soon as Brad had finished his pint I suggested we go. Just as we got up, the landlord came through a back door, vest on, looking a bit puzzled. I was sure the barman must have told his guv that he should have a look at their latest customer.

We were on our way to the little car park by then. Brad Pitt climbed back in the car and sat in the passenger seat, I was driving, so Ronnie got in the back. The landlord followed us, hesitantly at first, but gaining speed as I started the car up. I rolled the window down as I began to reverse, but I knew what was coming.

'Excuse me...' began the landlord.

'Yes, he is! Ta-ta!' I called out cheerfully and *bang!* we were gone.

That man must have kicked his arse from here to China thinking, *I've just had Brad Pitt in my pub. No one's gonna believe me!*

No – that's right, because Roysie's too damn quick for you!

The main thing was that Brad Pitt had enjoyed an afternoon just like anyone else might – and that he was never in any danger or likely to be bothered. And I knew how important that was.

I've had some of the biggest stars in the world – male and

female – bawl in my arms because they can't go out the door, not without people like me. So when you daydream about being a big star, be careful what you wish for! You may think having all that fame and fortune would be nice, but personally speaking, I wouldn't wish it on my worst enemy! It's not all it's cracked up to be.

It's got a little better in the years since Princess Diana died. There are still people who get exposed in the media when they've been doing drugs and that's their own fault, but I think there's less of the intrusive long lens techniques of the paparazzi now – and that's her lasting influence.

CHAPTER 28

A STRANGER ON LAVENDER HILL

On the fifth day of the fifth month of the fifth year of the century, as Prime Minister Blair prepared to get himself re-elected, I died. At about ten past eight, I drove through Clapham Common on the way to a pick-up. It was then that I felt the sharp pain going down my arm – sort of pins and needles. *My God, that's painful!* Typical Roy in difficulty though, what did I do? Rolled down the window and lit a fag, kept going.

I crested Clapham Common and came down The Avenue towards Latchmere Road. But the pain was on the move as well: down the arm... and into my chest. It felt like I was being crushed in a vice. I've taken some punishment over the years, but you could add up the stabbings and the shootings, and the boxing and the doormen fights and they would not come to anywhere near the agony I felt. It was off the scale.

Heart attack. I knew it; I just knew it. *Shit! I'm going...* And if I didn't find a way to somehow pull over in the rush-hour traffic, I was also going to have a car crash as well.

Looking back, I should have seen it coming. All the signs

were there: I was getting tired, I wasn't as fast; I should have known it was time to quit. I was a risk to myself – but more importantly, I was a danger to those I was paid to look after.

But the truth was, I didn't know quite how bad my health was – I just knew I wasn't feeling one hundred per cent. The edge was gone; the sharpness was gone. Yet whenever I felt aches and pains, I told myself I shouldn't be surprised, not with all the wounds my body's suffered. I put it down to muscle spasms – *whatever, just ignore it!* Well, now I couldn't ignore it, could I?

I controlled the car until I could bring it to a halt – outside the police station on Lavender Hill, illegally parked in a red box.

Now the pain was colossal. Unbearable. Gasping for breath, clutching my chest with one hand, I channelled all my strength into the other to push the button on the hands-free car phone. *Call the office*...:

'Bill... it's me...'

He could tell there was something wrong, but I didn't have time to play 20 questions.

'Bill... please. I think I'm having a heart attack! I'm at the junction of Latchmere Road and Lavender Hill. I think I'm going, Bill, I don't think I'm going to make it. Please, phone my wife. Get her to ring me.'

Even then my mind was going through the options, assessing the situation as if I were still on bodyguard duty.

It was pretty simple: I didn't have the energy to dial a second number and I guessed that Joanne would go to bits. Bill could sort out help and in the meantime, Joanne could phone me. I was unsentimental enough to know that my chances of making it were slim to nothing and I wanted to speak with her one more time.

To tell her I love her.

'Assistance is on its way. Please, guv, stay...'

'Get off the phone, Bill,' I ordered. 'Ring me wife!'

As the phone cut out, a white van went past and in my fear and confusion it seemed to me as if a man came out of the back of it – or around it? Wherever he came from, he was walking up to my side of the car just as the phone rang: Joanne.

'Darling... I'm really sorry, I'm having a heart attack,' I told her. 'I don't know if I'm going to make it.'

The pain was getting worse. I couldn't speak any more and I didn't want her to hear me go, so I made the decision to cut her off.

You've got to fight, Roy! I told myself. But that just seemed to make the pain worse. *Just give up*, came another thought, *it ain't gonna hurt so bad – it'll let you go, nice and quiet.*

I have no explanation for what happened next and I'm not even going to try and come up with one. All I can do is describe the events as they unfolded and you'll have to work out for yourself what, if anything, it all meant.

The man I'd just noticed had reached my half-open window and he stood there, looking in. I'd never seen him before but I can still remember exactly how he looked now: Mediterranean appearance, jet-black hair, a chiselled black beard. And his eyes, piercing blue.

'Look at me,' he commanded. He reached into the car and placed three fingers between my ear, neck and throat. He pressed, and as he did so, he said again, 'Look at me. It's not your time! They're coming; they'll be here soon. They're coming.'

I don't know how long this went on for. I was just about conscious and the man was still there when a paramedic arrived in a car, jumped out and sat in my passenger seat. He addressed the man with his hand on my throat – to a layman like me, it sounded like they were discussing the situation in medical terms. The medic administered a spray under my tongue, popped an aspirin in my mouth and told me to crunch it. He kept talking to me and at last, the pain began to ease.

The sirens attracted police officers from the nick. They closed the busy road, creating a big enough incident to be reported on the radio. Back home, Joanne was listening, knowing full well who was right in the middle of it. An ambulance pulled up with more medics.

'You're going to be all right, Roy,' said the one already in my car. 'We've got you now and we're not going to let you go. You just hold on... Why don't you thank this gentleman...'

He broke off suddenly – the Mediterranean had disappeared. The medic got out to talk to his colleagues and to ask the police if they had the details of the stranger who'd stopped.

'What man?' asked the policemen – they'd seen nobody. Nor had the ambulance drivers. The medic looked at me in open puzzlement. I returned his gaze. *What the bloody hell's happened here? Who was that guy?* It was the weirdest thing. I would have put it down to some hallucination due to the extreme pain had it just been me who saw him, but so too had the medic. And the two of them had had a conversation.

The medics ran tests that confirmed what we already knew: I'd had a whopping heart attack. Helpfully, the coppers said they'd put a note on the car but that I'd have to get someone to move it. *Typical old bill*!

St George's Hospital was four minutes away in Tooting,

but they took me to the Chelsea and Westminster and I was still in too much pain to point out that it was much further. I was wheeled in on a stretcher and the medics kept talking to me all the way down the corridor.

A man in a suit, with six or seven doctors clustered around him, was marching smartly down the corridor the other way. As I made eye contact with the suit, he stopped and had a discussion with my medics. What they said seemed to interest him.

'*Really?*' he said. 'Follow me.'

And he led the crash team into the emergency room as my family turned up at the hospital. But the pain was coming back. I remember the doctors cutting my clothes away and hooking me up to drips. Claret everywhere. I was covered in blood.

My brother was there and he was almost in tears.

'Fight it, bruv! Fight it! For fuck's sake... fight it!' he urged, as I moaned in pain.

I bit my lip and turned my head, looking towards the corridor. My eyes widened in shock as I saw the Mediterranean again. He held up a hand and, like a teacher telling off a child, wagged his finger – *it's still not your time*. And the pain started to ease.

But the spell was broken when the doctor in the suit addressed me.

'My name is Professor Pepper. I'm going to take care of you personally,' he said. 'I'm transferring you to the Royal Brompton.'

So, off we went again. I was wheeled out once more, into the ambulance and to the hospital round the corner, where one of the corridor walls leading to theatre was dominated by a massive picture of the professor and a caption explaining that he was surgeon to the Queen.

I would have laughed if the pain hadn't been so bad.

Why me? It never ceases to astonish me how these things always happen to me. Only Roy.

The Professor explained that they were going to take something called an angiogram. He looked at the results of the tests that the medics had carried out at the scene. For a second, he seemed puzzled. Then he looked at me, at the nurse, back at the papers. He had to check they were definitely taken at the time. They were. Then there was a pause.

'Do you understand graphs, Mr Snell?'

'Not really,' I told him. He talked me through the various lines and squiggles on the readout and showed me where the fatal cut-off point was. I was way over it.

'I'm not sure why you're still alive,' he said.

The only thing I could think of was the Mediterranean's gentle pressure on my neck. Maybe that had done something? Even to me, though, that didn't sound scientific. I explained the way he'd laid his hand on me but it didn't make any more sense to Professor Pepper. Then I said I'd seen the same fella in the other hospital and this time, it was the turn of Joanne and my brother – who had both been there – to look confused.

'What's he talking about?' They hadn't seen anyone.

I knew the results of the angiogram weren't going to be pretty but still I was in dismay when Professor Pepper told me just how bad it looked in there.

'I'm going to perform an op,' he said, 'but you have to stabilise first. I'm going to send you home.' He told me not to do anything more strenuous than lift the kettle to make a cup of tea: 'You'll be back in six weeks.'

Professor Pepper made me feel so grateful for everything he'd done that when he asked me if he could film my op for a documentary to be shown to other patients, I couldn't turn him down. 'I'll do anything for the Heart Foundation,' I assured him. Later, it went out on Channel 4.

He came to see me when I was out of intensive care and told me that things had gone well. Then he addressed the nurse. 'I know it's usually a struggle to get most people moving once they've had surgery and have been moved here,' he said, 'but your problem with Mr Snell here is going to be making him stay still long enough to keep him here. He's not a quitter – he's a fighter. He's going to try and do too much, too soon, rather than not doing enough.'

And he wasn't wrong. I was home within six days. Professor Pepper asked me if I was sure I was ready, but he knew that if he didn't sign me out then I'd just leave – he knew, because I told him.

Back in Sydenham, I was greeted by a big 'Welcome Home' sign festooned with balloons. I have to admit I had a little tear in my eye. It was not just good to be back – it meant so much to me to be anywhere at all.

Steve, my eldest brother, had died at fifty. He'd had to have an operation to have his leg off and it wasn't long after that when he had a fatal heart attack. I fully expected to go the same way. I'm still in a lot of pain. I do hide it quite well, yet some days I can hardly move. I've taken my body to hell and back.

It was well over a year before I returned to something approaching full fitness. It wasn't so much the physical side – though that was tough enough – but mentally, it took me a long while to get over the stress of it all. There would be twinges of pain as everything knitted back into place and each time I even felt the slightest bit of pain in a finger, I would wonder if this might be the onset of another heart attack. Took a while to get the mind around that.

But I had begun to reassess my whole life. I became so much less materialistic after being so ill; money meant nothing to me. I had grown to hate it because of what I had to do to earn it. All I needed was my family around me, a secure place for us all to live in – that was enough for me.

CHAPTER 29

BACK TO SCHOOL

The last person I expected to see in the chauffeur firm in EC2 was Tony Marsden. It was 2007 and I was looking for some light driving duties to get myself back into the swing of work. It only turned out that Tony, who I'd known from the circuit for 20 years, had bought the company.

'Well, well, well!' said Tony. '*Roy Snell!*'

'*Christ!*' I laughed. I'd relied on his chauffeurs for years and now here he was, running the company I was trying to get in with.

'I heard you'd retired,' he said.

'Yeah,' I replied. I explained about the details – the heart attack I'd had.

'Well, someone of your calibre's gotta do something,' he said. 'We can't have you doing nothing.'

'That's why I come down here,' I explained.

He thought for a moment: 'I've got an idea. We could really use your expertise here. I've got all the motors; you've got all the contacts... If we put them together, we could supply the whole lot.'

Tony worked the film and record industry, and I thought I could just do a bit of driving; that would suit me down to the ground. Before long, I'd got behind a wheel and I was ready for my first airport transfer.

I knew it wouldn't be long before I picked up someone I recognised from the old days. An employee of one of the big record companies was the first to recognise his chauffeur – but I could tell he wasn't sure. Well, it had been almost two years.

'I know you from somewhere, don't I?' he said at length.

'I was in the security industry for a long while...'

'Oh, yeah – Roy Snell!' he said. 'The bodyguard!'

And the word soon got out – '*You know Roy's back?*' Now, the thing was – Roy *wasn't* back, Roy wasn't yet one hundred per cent. Roy was just driving the chauffeur car, that's what Roy was doing. But they were nice cars – one of my favourites was a beautiful BMW Series 7 with blacked-out windows, all the gubbins. To be honest it was hard to resist the lure of the graft. No sooner had I picked it up from a place in Chiswick than the phone rang.

'How's the car?'

I told them.

'Good! How long would it take you to get to the airport?'

Well, that didn't take long!

'I dunno – about 20 minutes.'

'Terminal one,' was the response. 'A guy's been let down.'

I knew the client from years earlier when he worked for Universal. We got chatting and he was still working in the same place. They had a car company already, but they weren't happy with them. He asked me along to the offices that very day.

There were six Universal bigwigs in the boardroom and they gave us the contract to do all the artists for two years. And because it was all new, Tony needed someone who knew what he was doing. And nobody knew more than me.

My first job was Amy Winehouse, just starting out and a lovely kid. She'd just had a hit with 'Back to Black'. She had perfect manners and we got on like a house on fire – no problem with her whatsoever.

I also worked with some old faces like Ronan Keating. I would take him everywhere – gigs, TV appearances, record studios and radio too. Soon I was swamped with work and as busy as I'd ever been. Universal had so many labels that I could be dealing with rockers one day and then opera singers like Katherine Jenkins the next. There was such a mixture of people – an explosion of talent.

Duffy was just coming up then and she was really bubbly. We got on so well from the first time we met and she enthused, 'Oh, I've heard about you. You're a legend!'

I said, 'Well, I wouldn't go that far... legends are normally dead! And I'm still with you, just about, sweetheart!'

I noticed that whenever anyone phoned her while she was in the car, she'd speak Welsh to them. I joked with her that it sounded like she was having a right row – I called her 'the Welsh Wobbler'.

Like many of the younger artists, she felt comfortable with me around. They'd all ask me about the established stars I'd worked with over the years. They loved to hear the stories – I think it made them feel twice as important to know they were being driven by the man who used to act as bodyguard to the world's biggest stars. You knew you'd made it when you got Roy Snell looking after you.

Duffy was particularly fond of me. 'You know, Roy, you remind me of my Da,' she told me. 'I'm going to call you my London Daddy.'

James Morrison was another – he loved being driven by me. He always called me 'Uncle Roy' or just 'Uncs'. He won't let anyone else take him, such a smashing bloke too. We get on really well and he told me he can't wait to see himself in my book.

I think Universal gave me the up-and-coming artists knowing that if any of the youngsters started to stray a bit, Roysie here would pull the reins on them because of my experience. The kids wouldn't be able to get flash or big-headed with me – I'd done bigger stars than they'd ever seen in their life. *Don't even go there!* And from my point of view, it was really nice to be with them at the start of their careers, sometimes before they'd even had a single.

None of them got out of line – they wouldn't have *dared*! A few became a bit full of themselves further down the line, once they'd seen a bit of success, though. That always disappointed me, when they got a bit distant because they'd made it. I became part of their old life, not someone they wanted to keep up with. It was true that only very few of them were like that and I soon put them right: let them know they couldn't get away with that where I was concerned. It was always a shame to see it, though. I don't care how big you get, just remember to show bit of respect. I've always done that, and that's why I got on so well with Universal. I could call anyone there direct, even the boss; I dealt with them straight and they were the same with me.

As my health improved, I began to look seriously at getting back into the security game, but things had changed since I'd been ill. You couldn't work without a certificate from the government-approved SIA (Security International Association) and the only way for me to get that was to go back to school. *School? Me!* I hadn't exactly done brilliantly the first time around; I was dreading it.

I chose an accredited firm near me at random: Bright Security. They did the official licensing and they told me about the courses I could follow, which would lead to the equivalent of an NVQ. *NVQs?* I thought. *Here we go*! At least there wasn't a school uniform.

About 25 of us fresh-faced – or in my case, not quite so fresh-faced – recruits filed into the classroom. Our teacher sat at his desk working on some notes. At length, he looked up, but before he could start his welcome speech, he clapped eyes on me.

'*Oh my God!*' he said.

'*My goodness!*' I said, equally surprised. '*Mr Ford!*'

Scott Ford might have been chief instructor at Bright, but he had started his professional life being trained by me back when I ran my own college. As I recalled, he was a good lad, one of the few who made it all the way through my tough advanced level.

What was it they said about the pupil teaching the teacher?

'*Mr Snell!*' said Scott. 'What are *you* doing here?'

'Well, like anyone else, I got to get my exams...'

'What on *earth* can we teach you?' he said, wonderingly.

He made a point of introducing me to the rest of the class once everyone had got settled down. 'You may have heard of this man, you may not, but it's an honour and a privilege for me to have him sitting in this classroom. May I introduce you to Mr Roy Snell.'

And the whole class erupted. Everyone was clapping and cheering, and God knows what else, as if to say, '*Christ!* Roy Snell's *here*? We're studying with *him*? He's a legend in this game!'

The guv'nor of the college, Scott's business partner, dropped by that same morning and asked if he could borrow me for a bit. He had something to tell me in his office.

'Listen, it's an honour to have you here,' he said, 'it really is. And the fees for the exams are waived – to show our respect.'

They knew I was struggling for dosh, getting back on my feet after all the health problems. It was a welcome gesture and one less thing to worry about.

Back in the lesson, Scott kept referring to me. It got a bit embarrassing. He'd sketch out a scenario and ask for a volunteer to say what they'd do. If they got it wrong, nine times out of ten, he'd turn to me and go, 'Roy – how would you deal with this situation?'

By the end of that first day I had to pull him to one side.

'*Oi*, behave yourself!' I told him. 'I do not wish to be treated any different at all; I wanna be exactly the same as them. Please don't do this to me – I know what you're going to say, but at the end of the day I want to do this on my own merits. I want to be able to sit back and say, "No, I did this." If I fail, I fail. And that's it.'

But I didn't think too much about the possibility of failure. That was, until I took the mock exam home.

What the hell was this? The rules, the regulations, everything had changed with the introduction of licensing.

I couldn't make any physical contact at all with punters any more, not even a gentle touch. Much less sling them down the stairs or put their heads through a door. I had to *guide* them out.

I couldn't tell someone to get lost. I had to inform them they were 'trespassing'. I thought back to what we used to get up to and I had to laugh. I only needed to fix people with a scowl, point to the nearest exit and bark '*Out!*' *See you later*. That was it.

Not now.

During a fag break, Scott and I reminisced about the

heady days when anything was allowed. I think some of my fellow students were shocked at what we got up. The business I loved and to which I'd given my life had changed so much that I started to worry. Would I know the answers in the exam? I told myself there was no alternative – I had to move with the times.

The night before the exam even my JoJo noticed something was up.

'I'm really, really nervous,' I admitted. 'I know kids must feel when they sit their GCSEs now!'

For the first time in my life I was going to sit an exam... I felt so inadequate.

Even Eden noticed.

'Don't worry, Daddy,' she said. 'You can only do your best.'

The words were intended to reassure me, but Eden was my daughter and she was only ten. I was supposed to be the one looking after her. *I felt so stupid.*

Instead of skipping it all the time to work, I should have gone to school – I should have learned. How wrong I'd been! Now it had all caught up with me.

For the first time in my life, the barriers were down and I felt totally exposed. I'd faced terrifying physical dangers in my time, but I couldn't shake off the sense of anxiety and sheer apprehension about the next day.

The first exam lasted an hour and they gave us a thick booklet to work off. Sixty minutes. That was it! Already I was sweating. I struggled to work out the words. Some were out of my reading ability. I don't think even Scott realised that; he'd seen me in professional action over the years and never knew I had less schooling than he did.

What does that mean? I thought, as I flicked through the first couple of pages. *How can I break that sentence down so it starts to talk to me?*

What's this? What's the difference between the colours of fire extinguishers? You even have to know about how to control a blaze now! I glanced up at the clock. That hour seemed to be going very quickly and I was only halfway through the questions. *Shit!* I thought. *Just get as much done as possible.*

At last I began to see the other side of the panic and realised there were certain things I knew straight off – *ding!* That gave me the confidence I needed. Answers began to leap out at me. That one... that one... this one...

Some of it I could take from my years of experience. The examiners might dress up a section as 'statutory first aid' but they were only asking what it meant when someone was on the floor on their back with their arms out. *In my day, that meant the geezer was unconscious on the way down, son!* And I was correct! It was just that they didn't call it that these days. *I wasn't doing so badly, after all.*

Then you had to say what you'd check first in an unconscious person. Would you say breathing? A lot of people would. And they'd be wrong. First thing is make sure that *you're* okay. Have a look around. Is there anyone in the crowd who doesn't like the person who's gone spark-out? Because if there is, chances are they'll come after you if you go to assist. It's all about health and safety, these days – for the bodyguard as much as the person they protect; you can't just dive in.

By the end of the exam I realised I'd learned a hell of a lot. I was quite amazed. And I was thoroughly enjoying it, too, much to my surprise. And that was reflected in the result – I scored 93 per cent!

I was absolutely gobsmacked.

And following my success in the exam I suddenly

developed a taste for doing more of them. I never imagined I'd be addicted to exams!

I went for qualifications in controlling crowds and arena-management, security static guarding, door supervision – and I passed every single one of them. I was elated. And I was on my way back; I had self-belief and I put my mind to making myself work.

Okay, they were just certificates, I know that. And I know there will be people out there who can't see what the big deal is. A child could probably study to that standard. Fair enough, good point.

But for me going through that whole process of studying, learning, revising and sitting an exam was a major achievement in itself. I'd not tried to buck the system; I'd accepted the need to get the badge, fair and square. The feeling of winning was like no other.

With each new course I try and help my fellow students as best I can, taking them through common situations until they get to the right place by themselves. I have the experience for that, and I find I'm good at it too.

So, with Scott's encouragement, I plan to take an instructor's exam and teach alongside him. By then I will have done every course, ticked every box. I want to be able to do everything before I go on to tell other people how to do their job.

I'm hoping that I will soon be back where I belong – working alongside my buddies at Universal. And there's more: I want to get into doing consultancy and to work with Bright.

As I make my plans, I find my strength is returning and I've got more energy than ever before. I had been thinking about retiring, but it was never really going to happen. People tell me the work's been part of my life for too long and I've got a lot to give; they say that others can learn from me and I've come to realise they're right.

I've also been asked by a friend who works with the Prince's Trust to do some talks to schools, where there are gang members and kids who have gone off the rails.

'The kids will really listen to someone like you,' he told me. 'You've actually been there, done it and worn the T-shirt.'

We hope I can get children at a certain age – ten upwards, say – when at least I've got half a chance of getting them to listen to my life. I don't want to come across as a bloody do-gooder, that's not me. Children should be allowed to be children, whatever background they may come from. But some kids – and I was one – have a choice of two paths. The attractive one looks glamorous: a shortcut to the nice car, the jewellery and the cash, even if you have to cut a few dodgy deals to get there. The other path looks like it will take a long time, seems boring by comparison and you might never reach your goal.

But I can tell those kids that I tried the shortcut – and it did me no good at all. You can't escape it. I had to follow the long path. The alternative was a major prison sentence, a six-by-four or never knowing the happiness of family life that I have now. It just took me a long time to realise how to get what I wanted!

My greatest achievement was to discover what true love was when I met Joanne and to learn about unconditional love when I had the privilege of an uninterrupted experience as a father with Eden.

When I was ill, my brother said something, which for a while I thought summed me up.

'There's an old saying...' he began.

'What's that?'

'Old soldiers never die – they just fade away.'

And I felt that was appropriate for me. I hadn't died – well, I nearly had! Very close, a few times. And I wanted to fade – fade away into the background. That would have done me quite nicely. It was when I was ill and I didn't really mind, but now it's all different.

Now Roy's back.

An Ode to Roy Snell, Esq

Roysie is a big bloke of that there is no doubt
And he can certainly hurt a chap by giving him a clout
But the times they are a-changing and Roysie's not immune
You can read about it in his book, it's coming out real soon.

The contrast between Roy 'the boy' Snell of yesteryear and the Roy Snell of today is as great as an Arctic winter's night to a glorious summer's day, as the east of Kipling's day was to the west. What triggered the desire to change Roy himself relates within these pages but, as a friend, I can say that I have come to know, love and respect the man he has become and count it as a privilege to have him as a bosom buddy.

Gope Kamlani Jr (Junior – Wise Buddha)